MOUSEJUNKIES

Tips, Tales, and Tricks
for a Disney World Fix

all you need to know for a perfect vacation

Bill Burke

TRAVELERS' TALES
AN IMPRINT OF SOLAS HOUSE, INC.
PALO ALTO

Travelers' Tales is a trademark of Travelers' Tales/Solas House, Inc., 853 Alma Street, Palo Alto, California 94301. www.travelerstales.com

Art Direction: Stefan Gutermuth
Photo Credit: © Blaine Harrington
Interior Design and Page Layout: Howie Severson

Library of Congress Cataloging-in-Publication Data

Burke, Bill.
Mousejunkies : tips, tales, and tricks for a Disney World fix all you need to know for a perfect vacation / Bill Burke.
    p. cm.
Includes bibliographical references and index.
ISBN 978-1-932361-66-7 (pbk. : alk. paper)
    1. Walt Disney World (Fla.)--Guidebooks. 2. Orlando (Fla.)--Guidebooks. I. Title.
GV1853.3.F62B87 2009
791'.06875924--dc22

2008055467

First Edition
Printed in the United States
10 9 8 7 6 5 4 3 2 1

To Amy—I couldn't wish for a better wife, friend and travel partner. To Katie, who seems to have inherited the Mouse gene, and who brought a new perspective by allowing us to see magic through her eyes. And to Dorothy Burke, who was at the Magic Kingdom on its opening day, attended Epcot's grand opening a few years later, and who first introduced our family to Walt Disney World.

Table of Contents

Foreword

To look at me, you'd never suspect I harbor such a secret.

I live in a decent house, hold down a steady job and pay the bills on time. As far as you know.

I play mediocre bass guitar in a good blues band, I love watching football and I secretly yearn to trade my sensible hybrid car in for an unnecessarily obnoxious pickup truck.

But mention something as innocuous as "Main Street" and I break out into a sweat.

That's the first clue. Look a bit closer, however, and the signs begin to manifest themselves: Almost every shirt I own has a mouse on it somewhere; if you look closely at my watch you'll see cleverly hidden Mouse ears; I refer to the guy at the Sip-n-Go as a gas station cast member; and my credit card bill has an inordinate number of charges emanating from the Orlando, Florida area.

Spend more than five minutes talking to me and I'll figure out a way to insert Mickey Mouse into the conversation. It can be annoying, but I have no qualms about the fact that I am a hard-core Walt Disney World fanatic, and I know how to do it right.

This is not a boastful claim. It's just something I've learned while in the throes of my addiction. I love Disney World, and I'll spend as much time vacationing there as I can without going broke.

Actually, that's a lie. I don't really care about debt. I just need my fix.

I need to be standing on the sparkling clean streets of the Magic Kingdom, enveloped in ethereal music wafting from hidden speakers and bathed in the early morning Florida sun. I crave the oasis provided by an air-conditioned restaurant as fellow addicts fill the perfectly manicured park outside. And I need to end the day with a head full of frozen margaritas as IllumiNations unfolds in front of me—a majestic display of fire and hope.

But it didn't start out that way.

Falling in love with the idea of having my breakfast served by adults making minimum wage dressed as fictional cartoon animals was the farthest thing from my mind when I got on a plane with my wife and headed south one August day in 1998.

It was on that trip that I learned an important fact: Walt Disney World is not just for kids. It may have started out that way, but the days of riding "It's a Small World" over and over are over. There are nightclubs and restaurants and bars and attractions and shows and shopping and golf and fishing—enough to keep us going back for many, many years. For those who haven't succumbed to the seduction or haven't been to central Florida for a long time, it's hard to understand.

At first, I'd begin to plan a vacation and people would ask, "Where are you going?" Now, no one asks. When I say we're going away, I'll get a knowing nod or a chuckle. In fact, I've stopped saying that we're going to Walt Disney World. I just say that we're going to Florida. It somehow sounds a little less crazy to my ears.

I often think about why I'm so enamored of the place. I have theories about how working in the newspaper business I spend a great deal of time thinking about war and terrorism and crime, and how Walt Disney World provides a total escape from that.

That might be somewhat true, but it's too easy an answer. It would be best—and probably more entertaining—to examine how this all came out from the very beginning.

A Mousejunkie Is Born

MY FIRST FLIRTATION with Walt Disney World occurred on June 7, 1981. A collection of cousins, brothers, and sisters trekked from Boston to the Magic Kingdom. At the time that's all there was. Epcot's opening wasn't far off, but at that point there was just Main Street, the Castle, and everything that lay behind it.

We stayed in a motel that had a small arcade where my cousin and I discovered an Evel Knievel pinball game that had about forty credits racked up on it. As a twelve-year-old, that was about as magical an occurrence as I could hope for.

The memories of that trip are a bit vague now, and come mainly in impressionistic brush strokes: Riding Mr. Toad's Wild Ride, eating at a character breakfast at the Contemporary Resort, shopping at what would one day become Downtown Disney, playing on the beach at the Polynesian Resort and feeling like we had been transported to Hawaii for the afternoon.

Most importantly, I remember the feelings. From the minute we emerged from our first attraction—the now-retired Mr. Toad's Wild Ride—I realized we were not in a very hot and humid version of our local amusement park.

That's the primary difference between a Disney property and anything that attempts to compete with it: you can experience an amusement park, but you feel Walt Disney World.

I don't remember seeing Cinderella Castle for the first time. It's the icon everyone envisions when they hear the phrase "Walt Disney World," and yet I don't remember laying eyes on it for the first time. What I do remember is the effect it had on me. Looking back, I know that's when I first felt the power Disney would one day hold over me. During the entire trip we were always happy, always looking forward to the next thing.

When we returned home following the trip, I immediately went into my first Disney withdrawal. I daydreamed about it, talked to my friends about it, and tried to will myself there as often as possible. I had the Disney DTs.

The urge to return lasted for a few years. Over time the memories faded, but never really went away. With no return trip possible, I discovered sports, college, and aimlessness.

A lack of cash, stability, and any kind of personal responsibility hindered my dream to one day return to Walt Disney World, and I never pulled it off.

Time marched on, and after a few false starts I joined the rat race, met a nice girl, got married, bought a house, and embarked on a career in daily newspapers. All the while those memories would occasionally emerge, reminding me of a time when all my expectations were exceeded and of a place where there were no troubles.

It would be nearly twenty years before I returned.

From Chaos to Perfection

In June of 1998 I was ordered to take a vacation. I worked as an online editor for the *Boston Herald* and my supervisor had generously granted me an unexpected holiday. She had just returned from Walt Disney World herself, and her glowing review of the place was fresh in my mind.

It also began to rekindle long-dormant memories. I initially lobbied for a trip to Ireland, while my wife, Amy, pushed for Paris. Since we could visit reasonable facsimiles of both at Epcot, it was the obvious choice.

And that's how this all started. All the effort, the months spent in the embrace of the Mouse—not to mention the small fortune deposited into the wallet of the Mouse—began with a decision that took less than two minutes to make.

We began trying to figure out how to get there, where to stay, and everything else associated with a trip to Disney World. This was a bit before the internet became such a useful tool for planning vacations, so we went to a travel agent. I know that was a dumb move. Yes, I would come to regret it. But without this little diversion, our story would be a lackluster affair.

I told the travel agent we wanted to stay onsite at one of the All Star resorts—primarily because we could take advantage of the transportation system and it was one of the cheaper hotels on Disney property.

"No, you don't want to do that," she said. "Besides, they're all booked up."

Since this was, actually, exactly what I wanted to do, I asked our psychically-gifted travel agent if she'd maybe call and check to see if they actually were "all booked up."

She went through the motions and quickly hung up, saying there wasn't one room on Disney property for us.

We accepted that answer, but what choice did we have? I suppose I could've screamed "Liar!" at her and stormed out, but I only do that in cases of extreme fiction.

She then decided the Holiday Inn Main Gate East would be perfect for us. It had the phrase "Main Gate" in the title, so I envisioned a room looking over a stand of palm trees just east of Cinderella Castle. She just happened to have a package ready for us—airfare, hotel, and passes. She said we wouldn't need a car, since the hotel ran shuttles. Not knowing any better, we agreed to that plan. There wasn't much left to do but count the days until our vacation.

When the day arrived, we took the first morning flight and arrived three hours later in a place we instantly discovered was a different world. When we disembarked the plane, we were assaulted with a heat I hadn't felt in decades. It was a smothering, scorching, debilitating heat. approximately thirty degrees hotter than the face of the sun.

We picked up our luggage and found the shuttle nearby. We loaded into the van along with several other visitors headed to the same hotel. As we traveled down the highway, we began to see billboards advertising attractions at different theme parks. We started getting excited about the week ahead. The sun was shining and everything was looking good.

Until we arrived at the hotel.

Our home for the week was located on a main strip in Kissimmee. This was not the resort so lovingly described by our travel agent. Where was the Main Gate? Certainly not immediately to our east. Where was the palm grove? I could only assume it was behind the chicken shack I was staring at. Or, I optimistically surmised, I just couldn't see it through the heat radiating off the pavement, which smudged everything in my field of vision into vertical waves of blurry energy.

We got out of the van and walked into utter chaos. A mob of people was surging toward the check-in desk. Amy took the luggage and sat down on a couch nearby as I queued up to see if we could get checked in. While our trip so far had not been an arduous one, I needed order at this point. Even a line would have sufficed. Some civility, even. There was none. There were, however, flying elbows and stomping feet and threats bandied about with malicious abandon. Our travel agent failed to mention that we'd be arriving during Work Release Week for the Florida State Penitentiary system.

It was the only explanation for the pandemonium playing out before us.

After about thirty minutes, the mob began to disperse. I stepped up and presented our packet. The front desk manager issued our room key and provided a shuttle schedule.

When we first booked the trip through our travel agent, we were assured of two specific details: That the hotel provided frequent shuttle service to the parks—so we avoided renting a car—and that we'd be staying in a suite with a kitchenette.

The first thing we learned after checking in was that the shuttles ran once an hour, first come first serve, and they stopped running at 1 P.M. It was now 1:10 P.M.

Cinderella Castle was starting to feel very far away.

We grabbed our luggage and headed for the room. It was on the first floor, right next to the street. I unlocked the door and stepped inside. A hot, thick, stale smell hung in the air and there were flies buzzing about. The kitchenette described so painstakingly by our travel agent was, in reality, a microwave on top of a mini-fridge.

This was not good. I turned around to see Amy standing in the doorway, her eyes filling with tears.

I threw my suitcase on the bed, pulled out the phone book, flipped to the page with the Disney hotel phone numbers, and asked Amy to pick Sports or Music—the designations given to two of Disney's most affordable resorts. Given the disaster we were now facing she didn't have a preference, so I called the main number at Disney's All Star Music resort and explained our problem.

In a voice that to this day I swear belonged to a princess, the woman on the other end said our room would be ready, and that they'd be waiting for us when we arrived.

I silently cursed our treacherous travel agent and told Amy to grab her luggage. We were leaving this non-palm-tree-stand-having, non-Castle-viewing, giant, unruly mob at the front desk hell hole.

The checkout process did not go well. Suffice to say that the first person I spoke to was belligerent and entirely without the magic I associated with a Disney vacation. I was told I wouldn't be getting any money back (she was wrong) and that I was out of luck (I wasn't). I grabbed anything that might be used as a receipt and headed outside to catch a ride to our new hotel.

Approximately fifteen minutes after we'd arrived at that first hotel, we were in a van heading away from it.

In the process, however, a huge weight had been lifted from our shoulders. We really couldn't afford to pay for the Holiday Inn *and* All Star Music, but I did have a credit card handy and I refused to let our vacation plans go down in flames just because I wanted to stick to a reasonable budget.

Not surprisingly, this would become a recurring theme. Irresponsibility in the face of Disney was already becoming a hobby of mine.

Back to the van: Amy and I watched the lush foliage whip past as we began the final leg of our journey toward Walt Disney World. The feeling of elation we both were experiencing was probably from the not-entirely-accurate concept that we were pulling something over on the Holiday Inn people. We were splurging, and we were now truly just minutes away from the beginning of our vacation.

When we pulled up to the colorful front gates at All Star Music, the main doors swung open, swelling music reached our ears, ice-cold air conditioning enveloped us, and the cast member that met us referred to me by name. If cartoon birds had fluttered out to greet us we could not have been happier. Check-in was quick, friendly, and seconds later we were headed to our building. The bedlam of less than thirty minutes earlier was quickly becoming just a bad memory. I silently prayed a wish that those obnoxious people would be spending the week at Busch Gardens.

The room was exactly what we needed. It was small, but it was bright, colorful, air-conditioned, and quiet. My only complaint was that it was located roughly seven miles from the lobby. This was a small matter, however, and did not serve to lessen our newfound enthusiasm in any way.

We tossed our suitcases, snatched up our theme park passes, and headed back to the main building to catch the next shuttle to the Magic Kingdom.

I hadn't been to Disneyworld in eighteen years, so it was very much like I was seeing it all for the first time. We had finally arrived. We didn't exactly know what we were in for, but in retrospect we were just minutes away from beginning a love affair with a place that began its life with the unassuming moniker of "The Florida Project."

Template for an Obsession

At first blush, the Magic Kingdom looked much as I had remembered it. All summer the one thing I couldn't wait to see was Cinderella Castle from the far end of Main Street. We headed inside—just in time for the beginning of the daily 3 P.M. parade. My dream view would have to wait. It was crowded, but we decided to make our way up the righthand side of Main Street USA.

By the time we got near the Castle, the parade was getting ready to start in earnest. We veered right and headed into Tomorrowland. It was oppressively hot. There were so many people, and it had been so long since either of us had been to the Magic Kingdom, we had a hard time getting our bearings. We were lost in a world of bright colors, cacophonous sounds, and hordes of people milling about. Many of these people were wearing strange hats on their heads and exhausted looks on their faces. I would one day come to know that look well, but this was day one of a new obsession. We were primarily excited, disoriented, and sweaty.

We stopped just in front of ExtraTERRORestrial Alien Encounter, which, by the way, no longer exists, saw no line, and headed inside. It stopped being hot, and that was good. Air conditioning quickly became the measuring stick by which we gauged the success of attractions.

Trying to skip to the next closest artificially chilled enclave, we ducked into the nearby Timekeeper attraction—a Circle Vision 360-degree film combining audio animatronics and a humorous storyline narrated by, among others, Robin Williams. Until now, we had been going nonstop since about 4:30 A.M. This was the first time all day we had had a chance to relax for a minute and take stock of where we were and what had happened.

It was at this moment that a not entirely unpleasant haze began to overtake me. At the time I believed it was relaxation. In reality it was closer to euphoria. I began to suspect Disney was pumping some kind of synthesized opiate through its air-conditioning systems, and I liked it.

What happened next would cost me many thousands of dollars, consume countless hours of thought and focus, and bring a bemused disapproval from family and friends.

This is the precise moment I fell in love with Walt Disney World. It happened in the hallway leading to The Timekeeper—a rather nondescript attraction that has since been wiped from the face of the park. It wasn't the most picturesque spot or a classic attraction. It was a rather plain hallway stuffed with people, but that's where it hit me. My Disney love affair was consummated at this precise point.

We spent the rest of the day wandering aimlessly around the park with no real plan and reacquainting ourselves with a theme park almost entirely devoid of lines.

Almost devoid of lines. The mountains—Splash, Big Thunder, and Space—were a different story. We opted to skip them rather than wait for ninety minutes. Besides, our priority seating at the Crystal Palace restaurant was fast approaching, and my head was screaming by now. In the chaos of travel, I had forgotten to get my caffeine fix. It was a mistake I would not make again.

We sat outside the Crystal Palace and watched the crowd pass by. It was starting to get dark, and a bank of lights lit up the castle—first purple, then red, then orange, and then purple again. It was really quite beautiful, and the newly rekindled affection I felt for this place was starting to grow.

Exhausted after a day of travel, switching hotels unexpectedly, reuniting with an old flame, and finally stuffing ourselves at the buffet, we thought it was best to return to the hotel. We fought downstream against a steady stream of visitors heading upstream for the nightly fireworks display.

By the time we got back to All Star Music—the Resort That Saved Our Vacation—we were practically stifled by the heat, which made the icy air conditioning that much more satisfying. It was not difficult to drift off to sleep that night.

I woke up many times wondering if it was time to get up. Finally, it was.

A Vision of the Future—Circa 1981

In case we needed a reminder that this was Florida in late August, our sunglasses fogged up immediately upon leaving the cool confines of our hotel room. The humidity remained beyond my comprehension.

However, the scorching heat and crushing humidity served as not-so-subtle reminders that we were on vacation. We bypassed breakfast and headed straight to Epcot aboard the first shuttle of the morning. Driving by the Swan and Dolphin hotels gave me my first glimpse of what Disney had been up to since my last visit.

I had also never been to Epcot before, and didn't know what to expect. As we turned the corner from the parking lot and Spaceship Earth—the park's massive iconic structure—loomed above us, I got a glimpse of what post-1970s Disney looked like. Spaceship Earth is an 18-story geodesic sphere referred to by most people as "the giant golfball." For something that looks rather plain from a distance, it's an impressive gateway to the park beyond, and houses a thirteen-minute dark ride that serves as an introduction to Epcot's unique mixture of entertainment and education. It also serves as a great place to get off your feet for a while.

As a first time visitor, Epcot was a shining example of what Disney's Imagineers had been up to since construction at the Magic Kingdom was completed. It took advantage of newer technology, was laid out quite differently, and felt much larger.

We stopped in at the Fountainview Café and had a quick bite. I was determined not to make the same mistake I made a day earlier. Caffeine would be an essential part of the Disney experience. As it turned out, our timing was perfect. As we sat down to eat, the first fountain show of the day kicked off. I'm not one to fall for water shows or flowers or topiary—normally. I'd rather watch a hockey fight than a ballet, but I shockingly found myself enraptured by the dancing waters and the swelling music. I still couldn't really explain the hold this place had on me, but as evidence my love of a water show, it was tightening its grip.

It was almost as if Disney knew it had me, and now it was just showing off. Every new thing I saw confirmed that even though we were only now embarking on our first full day at the vacation kingdom, I would be back.

We wandered through the main plaza, and came out near Ellen's Energy Adventure—a lengthy treatise on different types of energy. Amy said she wanted to head inside, and since it was forty-five minutes long we wouldn't have to kill too much time before the World Showcase opened.

I protested, saying forty-five minutes was far too long to spend on one ride.

"But it's air conditioned," she said.

We got in line.

Not long after we found ourselves winding our way through the World Showcase, a world's fair come to life that loops around a scenic lagoon.

We planned to eat at Chefs de France that evening, and arranged to have our reservations moved a bit earlier. This would serve two purposes: it would get us in a little earlier, and it would allow us to order off the lunch menu—which in some cases is the same food, only less expensive. Our reservations sufficiently altered, we continued on to the United Kingdom pavilion.

We stopped on the bridge connecting the two lands and took a good long look across the lake. I wasn't prepared for the brilliant layout of the park, the perfectly manicured landscaping, the moving, ambient music or the feeling of happiness and relaxation that seemed to permeate the place.

When we arrived in Epcot's version of the United Kingdom, we headed straight for the Rose and Crown Pub. In another example of Disney making dreams come true, we learned they served Guinness. I was pleased. Then I was pleased again by the size of approximately one pint.

As we walked back across the bridge toward dinner, the lights encircling the World Showcase Lagoon blinked on and I fell more deeply in love with this small part of central Florida. We arrived back at France just a bit before our advanced dining reservation time.

They didn't want to seat us.

"We weel seat you, but we weel not serve you until zee propair time," the waiter said. Being in Disney, I wasn't in the mood to argue. We ate our bread and water and watched waiters stand around and watch us as we all waited for our appointed dining time to arrive.

Our table was by the window, introducing us to one of the finest people-watching locations in all of Walt Disney World, so rather than pick a fight we enjoyed a bit of down time. In the end it was worth the wait. The food was good, the service was friendly, despite the maitre d's obsession with time, and the ambience was immersive. Designed to resemble a French neighborhood with shops and a view of the Eiffel Tower in the distance, the pavilion completely took us out of central Florida and transported us to Paris—if only on the surface and only for a short time.

It was getting late in the day, and since we were both used to getting up at 4:30 A.M. we were starting to tire. Too worn out to continue the commando pace, we headed back to the Resort That Saved Our Vacation.

We filled out a few postcards and watched the in-room resort channel for a while before falling asleep later that night. I woke up several times to see if it was time to head back out to discover what else this place had to offer.

Eventually, it was.

The Heat Claims a Casualty

We caught an early bus to MGM Studios and headed across the parking lot. It was a sunny, beautiful day, but even at this early hour it was hotter than it had been previously.

We encountered a pair of cast members at the gate who inquired about our plans. They talked us out of our plan of attack, convincing us instead to fill a nearby stadium nearly an hour before show time. We took their advice, but later found it to be misguided. The villains were among us.

As we walked down New York Street a few hours later, the heat peaked. It had progressed from merely scorching and crushingly humid to incendiary and unable to support human life. We were both starting to falter a bit. At the end of the street however, I found the "Singing in the Rain" lamppost. It had an iron umbrella attached to it, and if you held the handle rain started falling out of it. It was a quick way to cool off, and I even drew a crowd. Since the sun had sapped my sense of humor, I just stood there looking menacing and getting wet.

After toughing it out for a few hours, we wavered, bent, and finally broke. It was time to get away from this blast furnace with movies. We surmised that an air-conditioned drive over to Disney's new Animal Kingdom park would soothe our scorched psyches.

The Rain, Rain, Rain Came Down, Down, Down

The convenience of the Disney transportation system alone made it worth the whole rigmarole that accompanied changing our hotel earlier in the week. As we queued up to catch one of those buses to Disney's Animal Kingdom early one morning, the weather grew rather threatening. As we made our way to the front gates of the park—our second trip there in as many days—it started to come down.

"It'll stop in twenty minutes," I confidently predicted.

Forty minutes later we found ourselves jumping over puddles and attempting to remain just a little dry. We were still reluctant to admit defeat by buying a rain poncho, so we ducked into a shop to dry off. By the time we finished shopping the rain had turned sideways. It was coming down so hard it was difficult to see.

This, I would come to learn, was how it rained in Florida.

We relented and bought two rain ponchos. When we went outside, I turned to look at something, turned back to ask Amy a question, and looked out over a sea of light-brown-clad people who—aside from differing heights and widths—looked exactly the same in their Animal Kingdom rain ponchos.

TIP *Bring your own rain poncho from home. It'll help you stand out among thousands of other tourists caught in a typical Florida rainstorm.*

By the time we caught the bus to head back out to Epcot later that day, the skies had cleared. Through some tragic accident, we found ourselves walking into the Journey Into Imagination attraction. Inexplicably, when it underwent two distinct overhauls in ensuing years, people were saddened by the excising of its small, purple dragon mascot, Figment, from this brief journey into boredom. I hated it. I hated the song and the contrived cuteness. I hated everything about it. It nearly single-handedly killed the Disney magic for me. It represented that point in a relationship when you learn something unseemly about the person you previously thought of as beautiful, perfect and unblemished.

As it turns out, Disney World had its own blemish. And it was called Journey Into Imagination. Had the attraction gone on for a few seconds longer, this book would've been quite a bit shorter—indeed, might have been stillborn.

Following the sickeningly sweet Figment, I was ready for a good, stiff drink. We walked over to the United Kingdom pavilion and headed straight for the pub. It helped to soothe the scars inflicted upon my burgeoning relationship with Walt Disney World by the creepy Dreamfinder, the red-bearded host of the attraction, and his annoying purple pet.

When dinnertime arrived we found ourselves feeling our way carefully through the San Angel Inn to our table. It was so dark inside the Mexico pavilion's restaurant we could barely see our food. On subsequent trips I would learn that this was a blessing.

Dread, Sadness, Regret—The Last Day

Anyone who visits Walt Disney World has to deal with it: the final day of the trip. Hours filled with happiness, relaxation, food, music, drink, and laughter (and, let's be honest—exhaustion, dehydration, heat, grumpy tourists, blisters, discomfort and crowds) are about to be replaced with the return to the daily grind.

Despite my critical eye, the place was winning me over. For the small cost of buying into the premise, we were seeing world-class entertainment, eating great food, and completely checking out of the real world. Any inconveniences—reservation mix ups, the uncomfortable weather, attractions that didn't quite hit the mark—were just that: minor distractions in an otherwise perfectly engineered environment. As far as I was concerned, there was no outside world while we were there. No news, no troubles, and no worries. The last thing I wanted to do was leave it behind. But that's what we were preparing for.

Anyone who's been to Disney World, assuming they enjoyed it, knows how the final day goes: you spend the dwindling few hours trying to squeeze everything in.

Fortunately, we avoided spending the last day traveling from one park to the next by sticking to a simple plan: We'd visit the Magic Kingdom in the morning and Epcot in the afternoon.

As we walked slowly up the middle of Main Street, taking in the great view of the castle, we came across a young couple at the Partners statue in front of Cinderella Castle. The young man knelt down on one knee and popped the question. His companion was overcome with emotion as a barbershop quartet—the Dapper Dans—appeared as if out of nowhere and serenaded the two as they embraced in this life-changing moment. Disney's grip on my heart was now...complete.

We walked around the park trying to take everything in. I felt like I was banking magic to get me through until our next trip. Of course, I hadn't said anything to Amy about a "next" trip, but I was already working on one in my mind.

As we turned around one last time and said goodbye to the Castle, I envied the people who were walking through the main gate on the first day of their vacations as we were walking out. It's not too difficult to tell the first-timers, and that's one of the things I liked best about the trip. It's all but impossible not to get caught up in everything.

After dinner it was time to head back to pack up and get ready to return home. The only thing left to do was say our goodbyes to Walt Disney World and take stock of exactly what had happened over the previous week. Namely: I had become deeply obsessed with the place. Expecting an amusement park, I instead discovered a place that made me feel something. And that alone was reason enough to want more. The sweeping music, the unmatched attention to detail and the opportunity to act like a kid again—without feeling out of place or strange about it—was an entirely new experience. It was small enough to navigate and yet big enough to keep us uncovering details and finding new experiences for years to come. I found a place with a tangible sense of fun, happiness, and discovery. And I knew that if I returned, so, too, would that feeling.

When we got home, I was still buzzing from this new vacation discovery. Within days, however, I would suffer a backlash I could not have foreseen. I began to fixate on the things we saw and did on the trip. One night I pulled a chair up in front of our computer and started to write.

I liked what I had seen, and I wanted more. Every day I missed the music, the sights, and the feeling of being in a place that is everything you imagined it could be. I wanted to go back, and it had to be as soon as possible.

The thought of returning so soon seemed weird at first. After a while, however, it became the only option I would even consider. I wasn't interested in traveling anywhere else. I wanted to experience that same euphoria I had when we first arrived on Disney property weeks earlier. Luckily, opportunities continued to arise. My career choice aided in my new obsession, and I would spend weeks at a time completely immersed in a world where every expectation was exceeded beyond my wildest dreams.

Meet the Mousejunkies

So THAT'S MY STORY. That's how I fell in love with Walt Disney World. I went looking for a few days off and I came home with a new obsession.

As I was to learn, I was not alone. There were plenty of educated professionals leading otherwise normal lives who had walked the same path. Surprisingly, people I had known for years were either undergoing the same transformation, or had been ensnared years earlier and kept it a secret. Having given in to my addiction, I was beginning to recognize signs of the affliction and I was spotting it among people I knew.

One friend wore a Mickey Mouse watch—a seemingly innocent fashion choice, but I began to suspect something. I caught another whistling the theme from the Tapestry of Nations parade at a cookout. Still another hosted poker night and when his music selection shuffled and landed on the theme from Wishes, the nightly fireworks display at the Magic Kingdom, he was the target of derision from the cigar-smoking card sharks in the room.

I knew better. Furtive eye contact confirmed my suspicions. My friends were becoming Mousejunkies—people who had fallen in love with Walt Disney World and sought to return there as often as possible.

We began exchanging e-mails in cryptic Disney shorthand: "Hey Bill—just made ADRs for the CP in the MK. Staying at OKW but will probably head to the TTC first. Hope to use DME. Might get the DDP but it's two credits for HDDR."[1]

And yet, I understood them.

These are the people that became the Mousejunkies. Each had taken his or her own path to the World, finding their way independently of the others.

When the smoke cleared we found ourselves staring at one another over huge chicken legs and Dole Whips—the dining staples of any self-respecting Disney addict..

Collectively they have logged countless hours in the parks, spent untold thousands on their habit, and accumulated a library's worth of information on spending time at the Florida property. They have amassed a level of expertise no Disney fanatic could come up with individually. The Mousejunkies are a collection of experts schooled in the art of vacationing at Disney World. Leisure ninjas, if you will. They understand. They get it.

These Are the Mousejunkies

MOUSEJUNKIE RANDY: An engineer, and the most experienced of the team, Randy sometimes answers to the name "Disney King." Seriously. It's his e-mail address.

---

1 "Hey Bill—just made Advanced Dining Reservations for the Crystal Palace in the Magic Kingdom. Staying at Old Key West but will probably head to the Ticket and Transportation Center first. Hope to use Disney's Magical Express. Might get the Disney Dining plan but it's two credits for Hoop Dee Doo Review."

Randy's claim to the throne doesn't come lightly. When he called recently to make a reservation, the cast member on the phone told him there were forty-eight separate trips in the company's database with his name attached.

And that doesn't count the dozen or so Disney Vacation Club trips he's taken in recent years, or the odd vacation or two booked under someone else's name.

"Why am I the Disney King?" Randy laughed of his tongue-in-cheek title. "I don't know. I guess it's because if anyone asks anything about Disney World, I seem to know the answer."

Randy lives and breathes Disney.

"I took my first trip there in 1993," he said. "Then I started buying Disney stuff, going to the Disney Store, visiting the parks multiple times a year, and then I started working for Disney. It kind of snowballed."

Randy worked as a cast member in The Disney Store one night a week. By day he'd help design defense systems for the U.S. government, and by night he'd help design Disney vacation plans for store customers. He pioneered pin trading at the store, and was instrumental in launching scores of first-time ventures to the vacation kingdom.

Possibly one of the more highly educated retail workers in the mall, Randy took his role seriously. His enthusiasm for anything Disney was contagious.

The way he describes it, going to Walt Disney World is like "living a fantasy. It's a fantasy brought to life."

It was on his honeymoon—with his wife, Mousejunkie Carol—that he decided "this is the place for me."

"Randy is an analyzer," Carol said. "He'll find the best way to do things. His research skills are ridiculous. People will come to him and ask him to book their trips for them. It happens all the time."

Randy can also keep a secret.

We were at Walt Disney World in early October with our five-year-old daughter, niece, and Mousejunkie Jenna. We were celebrating my wife, Amy's, birthday. We arrived on a Thursday night, and several times during the day on Friday I checked in with Randy by cell phone. I'd give him updates on crowd size, weather, and what we were doing, and he'd keep me up-to-date on the baseball scores.

He never let on that something was afoot.

Saturday morning started with our group heading for Epcot. It also started with a surprisingly early text message from Randy, who was giving me a good-natured ribbing for not keeping him updated as to where we were.

We valet parked at the Boardwalk resort and made our way to the International Gateway entrance. As we came through the turnstiles, I noticed a broad-shouldered man wearing a New England Patriots jersey and a backwards baseball hat in the distance. This is Randy's park touring uniform.

Stunned, I turned to Jenna and said, "Does that look like Randy?"

She agreed that it did. Only wasn't Randy probably sitting several thousand miles north of where we were standing? Would Randy and Carol be crazy enough to fly down unannounced and try to pull a fast one on us? We were determined to find out.

The rope dropped just as we turned the corner, and we were instantly on the hunt for the Man Who Would Be Randy. We hightailed it up the hill near the United Kingdom pavilion, and crested it in time to see a flash of red, white, and blue fabric disappearing into Canada in the distance. I whipped out my cell phone and dialed Randy's number.

"Where are you standing at this very second?" I asked accusatorily.

Randy laughed.

"What are you talking about? I'm standing in a northern province, you goof."

I explained to him that we spotted him walking ahead of us in Epcot. In reality we were far from sure that the person we saw was Actual Randy. We settled on calling the man Fake Randy.

"You're in one of the most beautiful theme parks in the world and you're spending the morning chasing down some poor guy just because he's wearing a Patriots jersey?" he mocked.

He was right, of course. I felt guilty for assuming that our friends would spend the necessary cash and go that far out of their way just to surprise us at Walt Disney World.

I hung up and caught up to my group, who were now pointing at something in the distance. It was a tall, thin woman wearing a blue windbreaker walking next to Fake Randy. Carol is the only person I know who would need a jacket in the crushing Florida humidity. I dialed Real Randy back.

"We saw you!" I shouted. "We saw Carol in her windbreaker!"

Randy's nonchalance gutted my excitement. He said he was heading out to the store, and made sure we were following a sensible touring plan: that is, heading straight to Soarin' and getting Fastpasses. I assured him we were. He laughed, tossed off a "whatever," and said he'd call later in the day with Red Sox scores.

The endgame was on. We picked up our pace and headed for the Land pavilion—determined to spot Fake Randy and Fake Carol, if only to get a quick picture to prove to our friends back home that we weren't crazy. We ran to the railing and scanned the crowd below for a broad-shouldered Patriots fan and his permanently chilly wife.

We saw no one that would explain our odd footrace across Epcot. No Randy—Real, Fake, or otherwise—and no Carol. Dejected but rationalizing that such a last-minute trip would be crazy, we headed for the Fastpass machines.

As I reserved a return time for our hang glider ride over the Golden State, I saw a blur of red, white, and blue, and a tall, thin windbreaker-clad woman coming at us out of the corner of my eye.

Randy and Carol—very real, very much in the clothing we had spotted across the park, and hysterically laughing—descended upon us from behind a passing crowd. We were completely fooled by two of the most seasoned Disney travelers in the park. Boisterous, shocked laughter brought several cast members to our group to make sure everything was in control.

We found ourselves explaining that our friends had completely pulled the wool over our eyes, flying thousands of miles on a whim and tracking down our exact location in forty-seven square miles to pounce.

There's never a routine Disney vacation when Mousejunkie Randy is on-site.

 MOUSEJUNKIE CAROL: A partner in an accounting firm by day, Carol will run through a brick wall to get her hands on a zebra dome at Boma.

Carol first traveled to Walt Disney World in 1993 as part of a family vacation.

"My mom bought us the entire trip—the whole family," she said. "There were sixteen of us on that trip. That's what got me hooked. That one time is all I needed."

Carol has visited Walt Disney World as many as five times in one year. That's five separate vacations. To a Florida resident, that may not sound like much. But Carol lives in New England. Every month or two she was packing her bags and heading to the airport. Give Carol a ring on her cell phone and you're just as likely to find her camped out on the World Showcase Lagoon awaiting IllumiNations as you are to find her running errands around her southern New Hampshire hometown.

"The thing that makes it great is that you're going to a place to be a kid all over again," she said. "It's awesome. I've always been a game player—board games, video games—and my whole family is that way, too. So for me it was like we were all these big kids going in to play."

The quickest turnaround between trips was when she and her husband Randy went once in mid-October, and returned again to celebrate Halloween at the Magic Kingdom.

Carol traveled to Disney's Hollywood Studios to attend the soft opening of the new Toy Story Mania attraction. While waiting for it to open, she befriended a cast member from Windham, New Hampshire.

When she returned to the park two weeks later— a roughly 1,335 mile commute—she walked by the same attraction, shouted a hearty, "Windham!" to the same cast member, and scored a pair of Fastpasses for her kindness.

While she may be on a first-name basis with Disney cast members who work thousands of miles away, it's not the theme parks that keep her coming back.

For Carol, a resort expert, it's all about where you lay your head.

"My favorite thing is how beautiful the resorts are," she said. "Pretty much any resort is my favorite. You walk in and they're all so spotless and meticulously landscaped. It's amazing."

Along with her husband Randy, Carol has stayed at nearly every one of the 32 Walt Disney World resorts.

 MOUSEJUNKIE J: An engineer at a nuclear power plant, J can cover theme park real estate faster than any man alive and has been known to fashion rain ponchos from discarded annual passes.

An expert in touring theme parks and planning meals at Disney's table service restaurants, J has been to the resort dozens of times.

All hyperbole aside, J breaks land-speed records while traversing theme parks. The first time I heard a sonic boom in Fantasyland was because J had priority seating at the California Grill and it was getting late. He can fetch a Fastpass at Space Mountain, grab a turkey leg in Frontierland, do a loop on the Roger E. Broggie, and get back to Space Mountain again before I even get out of the restroom next to Guest Services.

And while I may be particularly slow, I'm not the only one to fall victim to his speedy, yet effective, approach. For example: He and his wife, Mousejunkie Deb, decided to give a Walt Disney World vacation to several family members recently.

It became apparent fairly early that J's pace may have been too much for this group of rookies.

"As is accepted practice among most of the Mousejunkies, we always go to the Magic Kingdom first," he explained. "It is the original and, in my opinion, the most visually appealing of all the parks. No one can deny that Main Street and Cinderella Castle are not *the* best photo opportunities in all of Walt Disney World."

The group boarded a Disney bus and headed for the park. J was giddy with excitement at the thought of seeing the looks on the faces of his family.

"Since I go so often, I still get excited to see things," J said. "But going with people who have never seen it is a magical experience. I highly recommend it."

After a few Photopass opportunities on Main Street USA, J, Deb, and the group began the trek toward Cinderella Castle.

That's when J was stopped cold in his tracks by a request he had not anticipated.

His Auntie Flo, who is in her sixties and not the best walker, turned and asked, "How much farther?"

Flummoxed, J stopped, turned to face Auntie Flo, and managed to stammer: "How much farther to what!?"

They had six days of park touring to do with a bunch of rookies. The pace needed to be swift in order to see the high points. They were in minute twenty-three of a six-day journey and she was already tired. J reacted quickly and said, "I'll be right back."

The pooped group grabbed lunch while J doubled backed to the entrance and rented a wheelchair for Auntie Flo.

"I became her chauffeur for the rest of the trip," he said. "This may sound like a chore but it actually had a few benefits. Pushing Auntie Flo enabled me to keep up the pace I'm famous for. I could get moving with Auntie Flo weaving in and out of the throngs of people."

 MOUSEJUNKIE DEB: A manager in her professional life, Deb can navigate sweaty throngs with an unmatched efficiency and ruthlessness. But it didn't start out that way. In fact, her first trip—a family vacation when she was a teenager in 1985—had a few very un-Mousejunkie like moments.

Deb's family flew to Florida from their home in New Hampshire. It was her first time on a plane, and she looked forward to the break from the frigid New England winter. She arrived in Orlando, prepared for a tropical vacation.

It snowed.

For the first time in years, there was measurable snowfall in central Florida.

The family's actual vacation destination was her grandparents' condo in St. Augustine, so the Walt Disney World portion of the trip was merely a one-day itinerary filler while Gram and Gramp went to Cypress Gardens.

"We were clueless," Deb said. "We rushed through the Magic Kingdom to log some vacation hours at the relatively new Epcot. After wandering through Future World for some time, we deemed the park small and lame and left.

"We had no idea we missed the entire World Showcase."

Twenty-five trips later, and Deb is a much savvier visitor. She also counts Epcot as one of her favorite Disney destinations. But it was the first time staying on-property—at Dixie Landings (now Port Orleans Riverside)—that awakened the Mousejunkie in her.

"It was the full immersion in the magic and the theming," she said. "And never having to leave the boundaries of the World for a full week. That's what hooked me."

From then on the trips became annual, and then semi-annual. Then came the Disney Vacation Club, the golf trips, discovering the joy of planning a trip and eventually convincing other family members to join her and her husband, Mousejunkie J, on Disney World vacations.

When asked, Deb has a hard time naming the "lightning bolt" moment when Disney tapped her on the shoulder and claimed another addict. She lists off several possible moments: "The first time I rode Space Mountain, seeing

Wishes over the Castle, taking family members for the first time, seeing the parks decorated for Christmas, purchasing annual passes for the first time, or discovering the handmade chocolate chip cookie sandwiches at the Main Street Bakery in the Magic Kingdom."

She is sure of one thing, however.

"I like to think my favorite Disney memory hasn't happened yet."

 MOUSEJUNKIE JENNA: A writer, Jenna is a virtual library of Disney knowledge with an encyclopedic ability to recall even the most minor Disney detail.

Jenna's interest in Disney World is readily apparent. She has Disney mementos throughout her entire home. Wander into her cubicle at work, and if it wasn't for the bitter Michigan cold freezing your nose hairs, you'd swear you were somehow transported to the Emporium shop on Main Street U.S.A. When she goes golfing, she has a Mickey Mouse pouch on her bag. She has a DVC (Disney Vacation Club) sticker on her car. She's a walking, talking Disney convention.

"I don't wear it every day, but I have a charm bracelet with one charm for every trip I have taken to Walt Disney World," she said. Which may explain her unusually developed right bicep. "Whenever I need something to occupy my brain, I default to Disney trip planning."

And that's where Jenna's inner-librarian removes her glasses and shakes out the bun in her hair in slow motion. Trip planning is where Jenna truly comes alive.

"I have always been a planner and a list-maker, and my interests in subjects often turn into obsessions," she said. "I don't do things in half measures. When a friend and I made plans to meet for a vacation in 1999—my first trip in thirteen years—she soon let me take over the planning because I immediately began poring over books and the internet to find out everything I could. Over the years, I've continued following those resources and adding new books, sites, and experts and try not to let any new information slip by unnoticed."

"Think of me as a sort of Walt Disney World reference desk—I know a little bit about a wide range of subjects, but more importantly, if I don't know the answer to a question, I know where and how to find it."

 MOUSEJUNKIE WALT: Walt is a restaurateur who knows good service when he sees it. And he sees it every time he travels to Walt Disney World.

"In the world today, where service is really lacking everywhere, Disney still does a darned good job at it. Sure you can meet a surly guy who has somehow lost the magic, but it's not the norm.

"Two things I like about going to Disney World: Once I'm there, I don't even see the outside world. It's almost like you're on another planet. You're surrounded by Disney—it's all you see.

"The second thing is that people, for the most part, are friendly and treat you great. That stuff is gone in a lot of places, but Disney has managed to hang onto it. It's part of the culture."

Walt first traveled to Walt Disney World in October of 1978 with his parents, sisters, and cousins. The family rented a house in New Smyrna Beach, which is closer to Daytona than it is to Orlando. But one of Walt's first memories of Disney World is spending the day running all over the Magic Kingdom, and then piling exhausted into the car and falling asleep on the drive back to New Smyrna Beach.

Close to twenty years passed before Walt returned to Disney World. But he was not exactly representative of his family. His father, Walt Sr., went back in the early '90s. He caught the Disney bug and returned for the next five years in a row.

"I just didn't get it," he said. "I couldn't understand why he would go back to the same place over and over again. Of course, now I get it."

The first thing that struck Walt on his return was how much the resort had grown in the ensuing decades. The second was that Walt Disney World wasn't just for kids.

"When I went back, it was with two other adults. We were three adults and yet we had an awesome time. It's not just a kiddie destination—it's whatever you want to make of it."

Now Walt returns to the World twice a year. A Disney Vacation Club member, he and his family have nearly six hundred points between them. There may be Mousejunkies who go more often, but there may not be any that go with more style.

"I only go once or twice a year," he said. "So I stay at the Boardwalk, I get the Boardwalk view—I do it right. When I'm there I want to treat myself to the best I can afford."

But it's not truly about just splurging. Not really. Ask Walt about his favorite trip to Disney World and he's ready with an answer.

"The most rewarding trip, by far, was when I was able to get my family down there with my grandfather, and to be able to do that through Disney Vacation Club," he said. "If I could only go once in my life, and if I spent all that money on DVC, that one trip would have been worth it.

"We went with my grandfather, my father, and my nieces and nephews, and we were all able to enjoy it with him. He can't go now—he's on kidney dialysis and he's eighty-six— but it was just so rewarding. My grandfather appreciates everything in life, and he was so happy to be there. I will remember that trip for the rest of my life."

When someone books a trip to Walt Disney World, they realize fairly quickly that it takes a little more planning and expertise than a similar vacation to Six Flags might. And that's when the questions begin: When should I go? Where should I stay? Should we eat at Chef Mickey's? Is it worth the extra money for a fishing excursion? Where can I watch the football game on Sunday?

The Mousejunkies have, at one time or another, posed these questions themselves. And they've learned the answers by trial-and-error. They've lived the answers and they're more than happy to share their Disney knowledge.

And then, of course, there's me. I can be stumped. If you ask me which Magic Your Way ticket is the most economically sound option, I probably can't tell you.

One of the Mousejunkies can though.

But I can tell you what it feels like to hug strangers dressed in furry costumes in 100-degree heat, what backstage at Disney's Animal Kingdom looks like, and what it feels like to be "That Guy" at the Monsters Inc. Laugh Floor.

Mainly, I'm just a guy with an addiction and a need to get it all down.

Mousejunkies Travel

WHEN THE TOPIC OF Walt Disney World comes up, the questions inevitably begin:

"Is Walt Disney's head really cryogenically frozen?"

"Was Donald Duck banned in Finland because he doesn't wear pants?"

"Were you banned from Epcot because you didn't wear pants?"

(No, no, and no one told me there was a dress code.)

But the most common question may be: "When is the best time to go to Walt Disney World?"

Depends—do you want to eat too much, drink too much, or sweat too much?

Travel in October and you'll arrive in time for the Epcot International Food and Wine Festival. Spend New Year's at the World and you'll be toasting with more people than at any other time of the year. Go in July for Independence Day, and you'll get to see a special fireworks display but you may wither in the searing heat.

Almost every time of year has its benefits and drawbacks, but what people really want to know when they ask "When should I go?" is this: When is it the least crowded?

Tales of protracted wait times abound. When it gets crowded, it can become uncomfortable and difficult to get around. The bottom line is that no one wants to wait in one.

The answer isn't that simple. There are several details to take into account on top of the crowd levels. For example: What will the weather be like, what are the theme park operating hours, and what special events might be going on at the time?

Crowd Levels

Even the best laid plans can be scuttled by unexpected or unanticipated crowd fluctuations.

Amy and I arrived for a day of fun at the Magic Kingdom one summer afternoon a little after 2 P.M. We walked below the Main Street train station and ran straight into an impenetrable wall of people. It wasn't a crowd or a mob. It was a wall. We grabbed each other by the hand and threw ourselves against it. We knew there were hot dogs and ice cream waiting at the other end of Main Street, and we were determined to get some. We ducked into the shops when it seemed like we could make headway more quickly, and headed back out into the street when it became impossible to move one step farther.

We emerged at Casey's Corner, ate a snack and assessed our situation, which was not good.

"We are Disney World experts," I said. "This doesn't happen to us."

It had taken nearly thirty-five minutes to navigate through roughly fifty yards of humanity, and cast members were beginning to rope off the street for the afternoon parade. We were running out of options if we wanted to escape the human quicksand threatening to drag us under. Suddenly the hotel pool seemed a lot more inviting. I thought we might have better luck catching the train in Toontown and doing a quick loop back to the Main Street station rather than turning around and fighting our way back down the street.

Sometimes I'm incredibly stupid.

We dashed across the street and made our way toward Cinderella Castle. As we drew closer, we noticed that the ramp leading up and through it was also roped off. We veered right, crossed into Tomorrowland and started heading for Toontown—along with everyone in the park who wasn't already on Main Street, evidently.

I had never seen it this crowded. When we did get in sight of the train station, we could see the line stretched back into the street. We had no choice at this point, it was time to commit to a plan and live or die with it.

We took our place in the queue and waited. And that's where we died with our plan.

At one point a young boy began kicking Amy in the back of the leg repeatedly. Her eyes narrowed, her fists clenched, and I sensed trouble. I had visions of her mug shot on the front page of the *Orlando Sentinel*, and I didn't want to see our trip end that way. In order to head off what no doubt would have been the most magical cage match in the greater Orlando area, I switched places with her. He started kicking me.

"We're Disney World experts," I mumbled, somewhat disheartened. "This doesn't happen to us."

Four trains entered the station, filled with passengers and departed before we got near the front. When the next train arrived and the cast member opened the gate to let people board, someone snapped. The mass of people behind us abandoned any sense of decorum or order they had and bolted for what they saw as freedom: any empty seat on that train.

I caught what appeared to be a five-year-old in the center of my back as a woman intent on making this trip out used the child as a battering ram. I turned to look at Amy. She had joined the mob. Her eyes were crazed and her skin was bright red. She was breathing heavily and bared her teeth at anyone who came near her. But she was sitting in an empty row just yards from me.

The mob had claimed a victim, but we were onboard. Minutes later we were pulling into Main Street Station, completely admitting defeat and heading for the exit. The number of attractions we had gone on? Not one.

The Magic Kingdom had beaten us senseless and spit us out, all because we failed to plan. There are ways to avoid our fate. Such as: take a look at the calendar.

If you're most interested in avoiding long lines, this is when you want to visit, according to statistics provided by Disney:

> ➤ January (Avoiding New Year's Day, because that's just insane and only crazy people and Mousejunkies Carol and

Randy go then.) It stays slow until Presidents' week, at which point it gets very busy again.

➤ Fall, from just after Labor Day until just before Thanksgiving.

➤ From just after Thanksgiving until just before Christmas. Historically, the closer you get to Christmas, the busier it gets.

According to Disney, you'll want to avoid these dates if large crowds make you want to tear your hair out and howl like a Tuvan throat singer (or if you want to go to Walt Disney World and not see me):

➤ Presidents' week in February.

➤ Spring Break, from St. Patrick's Day through the end of April.

➤ Memorial Day weekend.

➤ The summer months: June through Labor Day.

➤ Thanksgiving Day and the two to three days following.

➤ Christmas week through New Year's Day

Having visited all times of the year, I've learned some specific times when crowds are at their lowest. The scientists down at Mousejunkie Labs have spared no expense in uncovering these recommended dates:

➤ The second week in January: Guests staying for the New Year's holiday have gone home, and it'll be too early for students with February school vacations on the horizon.

➤ The last two weeks in August: Schools in the Southern states are back in session.

➤ September: Despite the Free Dining promotion, all American kids are back in school at this point and the temperatures are still blazing. This keeps a percentage of youngsters away, and the blast furnace-like heat tends to keep the weaker of the species at bay.

TIP *Extra Magic Hours allow guests to spend more time in a theme park. Either get to the EMH park early, or plan to avoid it entirely. The EMH park will be the most crowded of the four Walt Disney World theme parks that day. According to numbers Disney has made available, the Magic Kingdom is most busy on Monday, Thursday, and Saturday; Epcot is busiest on Tuesday and Friday; Disney's Hollywood Studios is most crowded on Sunday and Wednesday; and Disney's Animal Kingdom's busiest days are on Monday, Tuesday, and Wednesday.*

There used to be a time when October was widely considered to be the slowest time of the year. Then word got out that the weeks between Thanksgiving and Christmas were great times to visit due to lighter crowds. Late summer had traditionally been a better time to go since most kids were heading back to school.

Those halcyon days of breezing from one attraction to the next while enjoying the holiday décor are gone. Disney has launched seasonal celebrations, special promotions, and reduced rates to coax people into visiting.

October is when the Epcot International Food and Wine Festival is held. Word got out about the Thanksgiving to

MOUSEJUNKIE RANDY: When is the best time to go? It all depends on how often you go and what you want to see. Even though we went on the Fourth of July, which is the busiest day of the year other than New Year's Eve, we were able to do a lot and see things you can't see any other time. We were able to catch the Fourth of July fireworks, which they only show for two nights out of the entire year. You just have to set your goals, know what you want to accomplish and not try to do too much.

Christmas lull, and guests were quick to take advantage. Additionally, Disney Vacation Club members take advantage of that time frame, since the point cost per room is quite low for the month of December. The past few years, Disney has offered a "Free Dining" period for the month of September.

While the crowds during those times may not rival summer levels, the parks are much busier than in previous years. There are better times to visit. Not necessarily ideal, but certainly better.

Special Events

Disney has a peculiar way of marking time that carries over to almost all of its promotional seasons. Halloween at Walt Disney World starts in early September. Christmas at Walt Disney World starts at the beginning of November. The

MOUSEJUNKIE CAROL: I like to go in October. Hands down it's the best time of year to go. Don't even give a second thought to any other time of year. It's not that busy, it's not that blasted hot and it's usually pretty dry so you won't get rained out every day. Plus, that's when the two best celebrations are taking place: the Food and Wine Festival and Halloween.

"Year of a Million Dreams" promotion was twenty-two months long, but "Almost Two Years of a Million Dreams" doesn't have quite the same ring to it.

As a guest, this method of scheduling provides plenty of opportunity to enjoy holidays and special events year-round.

The Epcot International Food and Wine Festival is a foodie's paradise. Guests can visit dozens of kiosks set up around the World Showcase and try sample-sized food and drinks from around the globe. Each sample usually costs $1 to $3, while drinks traditionally cost a bit more.

We visited the Festival armed with our Disney Dining Plan cards on a recent autumn day. The Disney Dining Plan is a way to pre-pay for your meals. Guests on the plan are allowed one counter service meal, one snack, and one table service meal per day. However, you can use them all in one day if you like. When the credits run out, you're back to paying cash.

We saved our snack credits and planned to use them all at the Epcot International Food and Wine festival. Each sample-sized tidbit would cost one snack credit. We started in the booth serving Greek food and embarked on a nonstop epicurean orgy of tiny food that would last into the night.

A funny thing happened on the way to stuffing ourselves. Each time we ordered a sample and handed over our Disney Dining Plan card, we would end up with *more* credits than when we started. The legendary Disney magic was at work, (or there was a glitch in the Disney Dining Plan system?). We sampled Japanese sukiyaki, French champagne, and Wyoming buffalo, to our increasingly cholesterol-blocked hearts' content. (Yes, I am aware Wyoming is not a country, but the buffalo-and-onion item was delicious, so I refrained from lodging a complaint.)

The Epcot International Food and Wine Festival runs from late September through early November.

Every fall, the Magic Kingdom is dressed up in its finest autumnal wear, as Halloween descends on the theme park. An entire decorative transformation takes place, as pumpkins, corn stalks, and orange and yellow bunting are put on display.

The main event of the season is **Mickey's Not So Scary Halloween Party**. A hard-ticket event, guests pay an extra entrance fee to attend the affair which takes place from 6 P.M. to midnight on selected evenings. A special Halloween parade is led by a live-action headless horseman. Guests often dress in costume, and can trick or treat at pre-determined sites around the park. At the end of the night, guests are treated to a special "Hallowishes" fireworks display.

Is it worth the extra $40 to attend the party? The parade is fantastic, the fireworks are brilliant, the costumes guests come up with are astoundingly creative and you'll go home with enough candy to keep you stocked through next Halloween. While there are still lines, they're not typically as long as you'd find during the day.

The Yuletide answer to the Halloween celebration is **Mickey's Very Merry Christmas Party.** Christmas—on the extended Disney calendar—runs from the beginning of November through New Year's. Guests take part in a festive extravaganza, where they sip hot chocolate and munch cookies as snow falls gently onto Main Street USA. A special parade (Mickey's Once Upon a Christmastime Parade) steps off twice nightly, and a "Holiday Wishes: Celebrate the Spirit of the Season" fireworks display is featured each night of the party. Guests must purchase a separate entrance ticket for the event.

Where the Halloween party wowed us, the Christmas party left us just a bit underwhelmed. It's an extremely well-organized, colorful and fun event, and it may be my thick New England blood, but it just isn't Christmas if I'm not kicking the slush out of the bottom of my wheel wells. Santa doesn't leave presents under palm trees around our house, and it's very odd to be sweating during a snowstorm (actually, soap bubbles shot into the air over Main Street.)

Where the Magic Kingdom falls just a tad short, Epcot comes through with flying colors. **The Candlelight Processional** is an annual favorite that has its roots in Disneyland.

MOUSEJUNKIE WALT: My favorite time of year has traditionally been October. There are several reasons for this. I am not a fan of waiting in long lines just to go on an attraction that lasts two minutes. Since October is so close to when the kiddies return to school, there are not many of them around and this is a slower time for the parks. The other reason I like October is the weather. It is still hot enough to enjoy the water parks, which can be a lot of fun and can be quite refreshing.

I have changed, though. December is now my favorite time to visit. I love all of the Christmas shows, the decorations and the music. From November through Christmas the parks are transformed into a winter wonderland. I love the Christmas party in the Magic Kingdom with snow falling on Main Street, the parade, the special holiday fireworks. Epcot is also amazing with the holiday shows in each World Showcase pavilion. The highlight of the trip is the Candlelight Procession. I get goose bumps watching this. It's such a beautiful performance that it really puts me in the holiday spirit.

First performed at the West Coast park in 1958, the Candlelight Processional and Massed Choir is a nightly event that runs from late November through New Year's Eve. More than four hundred performers take the stage to perform classic Christmas music and to back a celebrity guest narrator who reads the story of the Nativity.

The orchestra is made up of fifty-one musicians, while hundreds of choir members dress in colored robes to create a visual Christmas tree on a multi-tiered stage. Performers in red and black make up the base of the tree, while cast members from all departments dress in green to make up the tree itself. One performer, stationed at the top, acts as the star atop the tree.

At the beginning of the show, the lights are dimmed and members of the choir file in holding candles. As they take their place, trumpeters herald the arrival of the guest narrator (Edward James Olmos is a perennial favorite) and the performance begins. The power of the music and the depth of the story is inspirational and moving.

It is undoubtedly beautiful, but a curious occurrence takes place during each performance. Members of the military are taught to never lock their knees while standing at attention. Performers in the Candlelight Processional don't always follow this advice, evidently. When the choir takes its place on the raised stage and the show begins, performers will slowly yet steadily begin to pass out. There are always several cast members whose job it is to help the stricken performer. It starts slowly, but by the end of the night there are any number of singers who have hit the floor and are then helped off-stage. It starts with a wavering, then a swaying, and then the performer often just disappears between other singers. Two robe-clad cast members wade through the choir, lift the performer up, and disappear backstage.

At first we were concerned, but it seemed to be a well-rehearsed and normal episode.

Guests wishing to see the Candlelight Processional must arrive quite early, or purchase a dinner package guaranteeing a seat in the America Gardens Theatre. The show runs about forty minutes, and three performances are put on nightly.

For the bravest and most committed vacationers, **New Year's Eve** offers a unique experience. The parks are packed—often closing the front gates and refusing entrance when they're filled to capacity. Epcot, in particular, provides the most festive and diverse celebrations. Each country in the World Showcase is at its most celebratory, and as a park that serves countless alcoholic offerings, it tends to be the most wild.

MOUSEJUNKIE RANDY: I like to go to Walt Disney World for New Year's, regardless of the crowd levels. I enjoy going to Epcot where there are parties in the streets. There are special fireworks and everyone is living it up all night long. At the same time, it's not like doing the same thing in Times Square where you are forced to freeze with 6 billion drunks.

It's the busiest night of the year, bar none. But realistically you're not there to ride the attractions. You're there to see the different DJs and dance and see the special New Year's IllumiNations display.

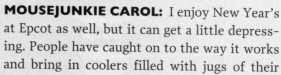

MOUSEJUNKIE CAROL: I enjoy New Year's at Epcot as well, but it can get a little depressing. People have caught on to the way it works and bring in coolers filled with jugs of their own alcohol. On one hand you've got families with children and on the other you have these massive drunks running wild over everything.

Its reputation is now well publicized, with one of the best-known Disney web sites advising guests: *"Arrive early in the morning and be prepared to spend the entire day."*

In fact, I saw one family there with two strollers—one had a baby in it, and the other was full of liquor.

A special version of "IllumiNations: Reflections of Earth" is presented twice during the night, and Disney's Hollywood Studios features three "Fantasmic!" performances.

When the holidays are finished and spring is on the horizon, Epcot blooms with the **International Flower and Garden Festival**. The park explodes with color as the largest collection of Disney topiary anywhere is surrounded by countless blooming plants and green spaces.

Expert horticulturalists tend gardens and provide tips to guests and special concerts are held during the run of the Festival at the America Gardens Theatre adjacent to the American Adventure.

The Epcot International Flower and Garden Festival runs daily from late March through mid-May.

Cost Concerns

Another consideration when deciding on travel dates is how much it's going to cost. Different times of the year are more expensive than others, and a sharp-eyed traveler will know when to plunk down the cash to confirm a reservation.

Disney divides the calendar up into their own five seasons: Adventure, Choice, Dream, Magic, and Premier. Adventure Season is the cheapest time of the year to visit, while Premier is the most expensive.

A room at a value-level resort, Pop Century, during Adventure Season will cost $82 a night during the week, and $92 for weekend nights. That same room during Premier Season will cost $129 a night during the week and $139 for weekends.

On the other end of the spectrum, a garden view, deluxe-level room at the Polynesian will cost $340 a night during Adventure Season, and $535 nightly during Premier Season. (Prices vary depending on the room's specific view and size.)

The seasons are divided up based on historical crowd size. The busier it is, the more expensive it is.

Here's a look at the different seasons for 2009:

➤ Adventure Season—The months of January and September, and Dec. 1-14.

➤ Choice Season—The month of October and Nov. 1-24, Nov. 28-30 and Dec. 15-23.

➤ Dream Season—Feb. 1-15, the month of May, June 1-10 and Aug. 16-31.

➤ Magic Season: Feb. 16-28, the entire month of March, April 1-4, April 19-30, June 11-30, the month of July, Aug. 1-15 and Nov. 25-27.

➤ Premier Season: April 5-18 and Dec. 24-31. (Spring break and Christmas.)

Getting in the Door

You're going to Disney World, so you're going to have to buy tickets that'll get you into the theme parks, water parks, and shows. The base passes are called Magic Your Way tickets, ostensibly because you can buy a base pass, or you can add any number of special options to your ticket. See? Your way.

Prices listed on the next page are based on Disney-provided information as of press time.

The Magic Your Way base ticket allows entrance to one of the four Walt Disney World theme parks. It's the basic "get me in the door" pass.

If you add the Park Hopper option for an additional fee, you can leave one park and go to another any time you want. Jump between all four theme parks all day long with no worries, outside heat stroke, exhaustion, and an overdose of awesomeness.

The Park Hopping option can be extremely useful. I'm a big believer in being flexible, and the ability to run from one park to another—whether it's to avoid large crowds, make dinner reservations, or to see a specific parade or show—can be invaluable.

Magic Your Way Base Ticket		
Days	**Adults, 10 or older**	**Children 3-9**
1-Day	$71	$60
2-Day	$139 ($69.50 per day)	$117 ($58.5 per day)
3-Day	$203 ($67.67 per day)	$171 ($57 per day)
4-Day	$212 ($53.00 per day)	$178 ($44.50 per day)
5-Day	$215 ($43.00 per day)	$179 ($35.80 per day)
6-Day	$217 ($36.17 per day)	$181.02 ($30.17 per day)
7-Day	$219 ($31.29 per day)	$182 ($26.00 per day)

Base ticket prices, with Park Hopper option added		
Days	**Adults, 10 or older**	**Children 3-9**
1-Day	$116	$105
2-Day	$184	$162
3-Day	$248	$216
4-Day	$257	$223
5-Day	$260	$224
6-Day	$262	$226
7-Day	$264	$227

Add the Water Park Fun and More option, and you can hit the Typhoon Lagoon or Blizzard Beach water parks, DisneyQuest, or the Wide World of Sports complex. If you're big on water parks or interested in the virtual games at DisneyQuest, it might be worth it. But I've never known

Base ticket, with Water Park Fun and More option added		
Days	**Adults, 10 or older**	**Children 3-9**
1-Day	$121	$110
2-Day	$189	$167
3-Day	$253	$221
4-Day	$262	$228
5-Day	$265	$229
6-Day	$267	$231
7-Day	$269	$232

anyone to pick this option so they could visit the Wide World of Sports complex—where many youth sports tournaments are held.

Add the No Expiration option, and unused days on your tickets never expire. If you purchase a seven day pass and only go to the parks for four days, you can hold on to those tickets and use them on your next visit.

For big spenders, spring for the Premium ticket. It includes every option: Park Hopper, Water Park and More Fun, and the No Expiration Option.

Being a Mousejunkie, however, we tend to opt for the Annual Pass. This accomplishes two things: It allows us to park hop and not worry about the number of days we should buy tickets for, and it ensures we'll return to Walt Disney World at least one more time in the calendar year.

An Annual Pass costs $469 for adults 10 and older, and $414 for children 3-9. You can purchase the Annual Pass at

Base ticket, with No Expiration option added		
Days	**Adults, 10 or older**	**Children 3-9**
1-Day	N/A	N/A
2-Day	$154	$132
3-Day	$223	$191
4-Day	$257	$223
5-Day	$275	$239
6-Day	$282	$246
7-Day	$314	$277

Magic Your Way Premium			
Days	**Adults, 10 or older**	**Children 3-9**	**Option visits**
1-Day	Not available	Not available	Not available
2-Day	$249	$227	2 Visits
3-Day	$318	$286	3 Visits
4-Day	$352	$318	4 Visits
5-Day	$370	$334	5 Visits
6-Day	$377	$341	6 Visits
7-Day	$409	$372	7 Visits

any time, and activate it when you get to a theme park. From that moment, you have one calendar year to come and go as you please. The rule of thumb is this: If you're going to be going to theme parks for 11 days or more in one year, it make financial sense to get an Annual Pass.

It also allows special access to sneak previews and special events held throughout the year. Annual Passholders often get to check out new attractions before others. It gives Disney a chance to soft launch something new, and offer a little extra value to Annual Passholders.

Passholders can also take advantage of discounted room rates, which vary from resort to resort, and have limited availability. Annual Pass room discount rates are usually ferreted out and posted online by sharp-eyed Mousejunkies, giving you a bit of a head start on getting that cheaper room. Also, calling 407-WDISNEY can put you in touch with someone who can provide availability information. Rates and dates often change.

Moving Forward

Once you're there, you may want to take advantage of a system Disney has in place to cut down on line wait times. **Disney's Fastpass** is a virtual queuing system wherein guests insert their park tickets into a kiosk that then distributes a small ticket with a return time stamped on it. Guests return to that specific attraction at the prescribed time, thus bypassing the sometimes lengthy standby line. Guests are allowed to have only one Fastpass per park ticket at one time.

For example: A guest inserts a park ticket into the Fastpass machine at Peter Pan's Flight and receives a return time for 1 P.M. He then immediately walks to Mickey's PhilharMagic and attempts to get a second Fastpass using that same park ticket. Instead of issuing a second Fastpass to the guest, the kiosk will spit out a ticket with information explaining when that guest can obtain a second Fastpass—usually when the original start time has passed or two hours after the original Fastpass was distributed, whichever is earliest.

It can be a great timesaver, and it certainly results in less time spent standing in line, but it can also mean crisscrossing the park in an inefficient manner just to hit designated Fastpass return times.

A Few Questions That Come Up From Time to Time

How do I buy a Fastpass? Fastpasses are not part of the ticket price structure. They cannot be purchased. They are free, pending availability.

Can you save money by purchasing discounted Magic Your Way tickets? It is possible, but savings are limited. The most important thing to consider is buying from a legitimate source. Stories of families arriving at the theme park gate with counterfeit, expired, or used-up tickets are legion, and there is no recourse. Never buy Disney park passes from eBay, Craigslist, or roadside shacks. Don't buy partially used tickets. Stick to reliable ticket brokers like Undercover Tourist or the Kissimmee Wal-Mart, which offers slightly discounted passes. They won't mail them to you, so if you want to take advantage you'll have to show up in person. They also don't have every ticket option at all times. While the ticket you want may not be available, a trip to neighboring Kissimmee might be worth it to save a few dollars.

Discounts can also be had for active or retired military, AAA members, Florida residents, and Disney Vacation Club members.

Whither the Weather

The final element to consider when choosing a travel time-frame is the ever-changing, usually extreme weather. Guests need to decide if they want to deal with scorching heat, drenching rains, or unpredictable and potentially chilly nights.

An interesting thing about the weather in central Florida: Just because it's raining at Disney's Animal Kingdom doesn't mean it's raining at Epcot. In fact, while it might be soaking in Frontierland, Tomorrowland may be sunny and dry.

Rain storms are frequent and often fast moving. While there may be days that are complete washouts, quite often the rainfall is predictable and temporary.

Here's a look at the monthly temperature averages, according to Intellicast.com:

January—72 degrees
February—74 degrees
March—79 degrees
April—83 degrees
May—88 degrees
June—91 degrees
July—92 degrees
August—92 degrees
September—90 degrees

October—85 degrees
November—79 degrees
December—73 degrees

The heat can often be bearable until the summer months when the humidity arrives. Even then, most of the theme park queues are covered by awnings or are inside and air-conditioned.

Then there's the rain. It's possible to go an entire vacation without seeing a drop of precipitation. But into every life a little rain must fall.

In the summer you can set your watch by the twenty-minute showers every afternoon. In the winter it's a lot dryer. Here's a look at the average rainfall in the Orlando area in inches:

Jan.	Feb.	March	April	May	June
2.3"	3.0"	3.3"	1.8"	3.6"	7.3"

July	Aug.	Sept.	Oct.	Nov.	Dec.
7.3"	6.8"	6.0"	2.4"	2.3"	2.3"

Perhaps the question, "When should I go?" is best answered with more questions: "Is cost a concern?" "Is weather a concern?" "Do you want to experience special events?"

But rather than duck the question, I'll answer it directly: You'll find me at Walt Disney World two times during the year for sure—late January and in October. January will be cooler and less crowded, and October offers Halloween festivities and additional food choices at the Food and Wine Festival.

And as far as I'm concerned Disney World is primarily a place to eat.

Mousejunkies Sleep

IT'S A MEDICAL FACT THAT some people suffering a sudden blow to the head are never quite the same. Head trauma can cause brain damage and permanent mental impairment.

I think it's these people who choose to stay off-site while visiting Walt Disney World. Staying off-site can be cheaper, and I'm sure people who stay off-site have wonderful vacations. Jut not as wonderful as mine.

When I step off the plane at the Orlando International Airport, I want to get to our resort as quickly as possible and bury myself in Disney for a week without coming up for air. Staying on-site allows guests to mainline the magic. You are completely immersed in that ambience twenty-four hours a day, for your entire stay.

I don't want to drive the wrong way under the welcoming arch until it's time to go home. I'm not interested in seeing fast food restaurants along the highway or visiting Wal Mart, Publix, Hooters, or Target. (Maybe Hooters.) But for the most part I do not want to be reminded that there is a real world outside the gates of Walt Disney World. And by staying on-site, I am allowed, for a brief time, to forget about the day-to-day hassles and real life worries associated with life away from my vacation destination of choice.

My one experience in an off-site hotel during a Walt Disney World vacation made me question the sanity of anyone who would voluntarily plant their flag outside the warm embrace of the purple signs. It was among the most horrific forty-five minutes I've spent in the state of Florida, and I would not attempt to repeat it. (For a complete account of this experience, see Chapter 1.)

The only other time I stayed off-site was at an International Drive hotel for a forensics convention. The room was fine, but the gap between the bottom of the door and the floor had to have been two inches. Daylight clearly shone through. And if sunlight could get in, then snakes could get in. I was convinced I would be attacked by one of the famous Jumping Snakes of Orlando during the night. (A breed of my own creation, since I am nothing less than irrational when it comes to snakes.)

I stuffed a towel under the door and spent much of the night listening for snakes. Which begs the question: How does one listen for snakes?

Regardless, I was convinced that if I was laying my head in a Disney resort not five minutes away, the Jumping Snakes of Orlando would not be a concern.

My point is very simple: Stay on-site. Staying on-site— at one of the Disney-owned resorts—opens up a wide range of perks not available to those unfortunate to choose a resort outside the confines of Walt Disney World. In addition, it allows access to Disney's transportation system—which means you save on a rental car. Off-site hotels also offer shuttle service, but I've found it to be first-come, first-serve (read: pushing, waiting in line, sitting in the middle of a parking lot for a van to arrive and traveling on their schedule).

Disney's buses are clean, normally run on a fifteen- to twenty-minute schedule and sometimes include driver-provided spiels that include trivia and entertainment for the duration of your trip. (Though this is less common now with the addition of an automated audio information system.)

Disney separates its hotels into three categories: Value, moderate, and deluxe. Prices, predictably, range wildly depending on a room's view, size, and the time of year you're traveling. As always, call 1-407-WDISNEY for the most up-to-date rates.

The value resorts are the least expensive and offer the fewest amenities. You won't find a sit-down restaurant at a value resort, but there are food courts. And while they are colorful and clean, the rooms are smaller and a bit more Spartan. Rack rates range from $82 to $160 for a standard room. Suites at the All Star Music resort, which sleep up to six people, range from $184 to $327 depending on season. **Disney's value resorts:** All Star Music, All Star Movies, All Star Sports, and Pop Century.

The moderate resorts offer a bit more for the price—larger, nicer rooms, and a restaurant option. A standard room at a moderate resort runs from $149 to $219, depending on season. However, there are more options—water view and pirate-themed rooms at the Caribbean Beach Resort, for example. The pirate-themed room with a water view will run between $199 and $274. Suites at Coronado Springs can run anywhere from $970 to $1,290 a night. **Disney's moderate resorts:** Caribbean Beach Resort, Port Orleans French Quarter, Port Orleans Riverside, and Coronado Springs.

The deluxe-level resorts, and I can only presume you're following the trend here, is top-shelf all around. Beautiful pools, top-quality restaurants, and large, comfortable rooms. The Grand Floridian, where people resembling Thurston and Lovey Howell and the odd Arab oil baron can be spotted, also offers its own spa. **Disney's deluxe resorts:** Animal Kingdom Lodge, Beach Club Resort, Boardwalk Resort, Contemporary Resort, Grand Floridian Resort and Spa, Polynesian Resort, Wilderness Lodge, and Yacht Club Resort.

Prices at Disney's deluxe resorts range from a first-born to a left arm. A standard room, depending on time of year, can run from $240 to $405 a night. However, there are a myriad of options at the top. Various suite sizes and views can push the prices to $2,700 a night.

Where to Stay?

Choose your hotel wisely—it can alter the feel of your entire vacation. I've stayed at each level of Disney's hotels, from Pop Century to The Boardwalk Resort. Each person's needs and requirements are different, which makes a blanket recommendation impossible. There are a number of elements to take into account when choosing a hotel.

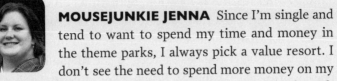

MOUSEJUNKIE JENNA Since I'm single and tend to want to spend my time and money in the theme parks, I always pick a value resort. I don't see the need to spend more money on my resort and room because I am not going to spend much time there. Instead, I put my vacation budget toward things like spa visits and tours.

For example, while the deluxe resorts are certainly top-notch in every respect, the amount of time you spend in your room may not equal the amount of money you might spend for the little extras. The rooms in Disney's value resorts—Pop Century and the All Star Movies, Music and Sports Resorts—are a bit smaller, but the hotels retain the characteristic Disney theming, cleanliness, service, and transportation options.

TIP *If you are staying at an on-site resort, take advantage of the package delivery service. Purchase anything at any of the four theme parks or Downtown Disney, and you can have your packages sent to your resort. The packages normally arrive at your home resort twenty-four hours after the purchase.*

Even after dozens of trips I still find myself back at a value-level resort from time to time, and I never find myself grousing about it. Still, there are a few hard-and-fast rules that apply universally: Namely, the biggest perk associated

with the costlier resorts is location. Something on the monorail line—the Contemporary Resort, the Polynesian Resort, or
the Grand Floridian—will set you back several hundred dollars a night, but offer the best access to the Magic Kingdom

The Boardwalk, Disney's Beach Club Resort, and the
Yacht Club Resort all offer walking-distance access to
Epcot's International Gateway (the back door into the park).
Disney's Hollywood Studios is also a quick boat ride away
from the Epcot area resorts.

As you might guess, Disney's Animal Kingdom Lodge offers
the most convenient access to Disney's Animal Kingdom, but
don't be fooled into thinking you can walk there. Transport
to the theme park still requires a quick bus ride.

If money is an issue, stay at the value-level resorts off-
season. Annual pass holders enjoy more savings, as do AAA
members.

TIP *As soon as you know the dates of your vacation, call
Disney central reservations (1-407-WDISNEY) and request
the AAA room-only rate. Depending on season and class of
resort, you can expect a 10–20 percent discount on rooms as
a AAA member. When the vacation date gets closer, deeper
discounts sometimes crop up. Annual Passholders can also
enjoy additional discounts. Using every edge, guests can
sometimes score up to 45 percent off rack rate, so the savings
can be fantastic. However, the discounts fluctuate and aren't
always available. Persistence is the key.*

Sometimes, however, saving a little extra money doesn't
matter.

MOUSEJUNKIE WALT Beyond trying to save Disney Vacation Club points (a timeshare-like lodging option where guests purchase a real estate interest), I don't really care about saving money. I'm not very good at trying to save money anyway. When I go, I want to go as big as I can while still being able to afford it. Sometimes people will ask, "Why do you splurge on the Boardwalk-view when it costs so much more than a normal view room?" The answer is because I like it! I say if you like it, go for it.

Here's a closer look at the Disney resorts various Mouse-junkies and I have stayed at in recent years:

All Star Music/Sports/Movies

The Basics: The All Star resorts are among Disney's least expensive on-site options. Each of the three resorts have 1,920 rooms divided into several themed buildings. The décor of each resort reflects its name. They are clean, bright, exciting places to stay. And at the low end of the Disney resort price scale, they can serve as a great option for anyone looking to stay on-site without breaking the bank. Each of the All Star resorts are virtually identical aside from the theming. *(Rack rates for the All Star value resorts range from $82 to $151 a night.)*

The Real Deal: I will always have a soft spot in my heart for Disney's All Star Music Resort. It plucked me from the jaws of vacation destruction and held me close to its (admittedly plastic, loud, and garishly fun) bosom. The pools are plentiful and huge, the food court offers a wide variety of choices at any meal time, and there's a bar just outside the main building. Plus, there's a picture of Carol Channing in the lobby. You can't go wrong with Carol Channing.

Pop Century

The Basics: Despite having a lower rack rate, Pop Century remains thoroughly Disney. A colorful exterior leads visitors in to a sparkling lobby that immediately reflects the hotel's given name: Pop culture items from the '50s through the late '90s decorate the walls, often slowing the check-in process as people point to items, exclaiming, "I had that!" (For me it was a *Circus* music magazine from the early '80s that featured both Fee Waybill and Angus Young, among others, on the cover.)

Check-in was a breeze, and before long we were walking toward our room. The expansive lobby—this seems to be a trend at Disney World—leads to a huge pool area, around which exceptionally bright four-story buildings are located. Forty-foot-high yo-yos, bowling pins, and Play-Doh icons add a playful touch to the theming, making it a fascinating place for kids. There are a number of pools throughout the property, and the food court is sure to please any child. Peanut butter-and-fluff sandwiches on blue, green, and yellow dyed bread, meatball subs, and macaroni and cheese are among the comfort foods offered here.

The rooms are smaller than those at the higher-end resorts, but not alarmingly so. They are clean, colorful, and again, a perfect place for children given the bold, cartoonlike landscape.

Located near Disney's Hollywood Studios, Pop Century opened to the public in 2003. *(Rack rates for Pop Century range from $82 to $151 a night.)*

The Real Deal: I had the opportunity to go on a personal guided tour of the Pop Century resort before it opened for business. I got to see a Disney hotel as few people ever do—completely empty.

My guide and I walked into the long lobby and I immediately felt as if I was in the movie *Omega Man* (or, if it had been 2007, *I Am Legend.*) That is to say that it was completely deserted. The lights were on and everything had power, but there was not a human in sight. It was a little disconcerting. Needless to say, the gift shop was not open.

The next time I set foot in Pop Century it was a bustling resort, humming with activity. And yet I was still reluctant to embrace the intentional kitsch of it all. Perhaps it was a cruel trick, but I was on a press junket that first placed us in Disney's Boardwalk Resort—a superlative hotel by any standard—and then moved to Pop Century. The purpose was to publicize the different levels of accommodations available to guests. But going from the penthouse to the first floor may have colored the way I saw this particular hotel.

The rooms are smaller, but I already knew that. We were put in a room on the first floor of the first building, right next to the main pool. I thought this was great, because it meant a much shorter walk to the food court, buses, and the lobby.

I enjoyed our enviable room location until 2 A.M., when a team of morning radio DJs, also on the publicity junket, opted to start their shift early, treating everyone within earshot to a

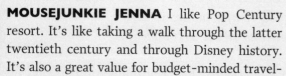

MOUSEJUNKIE JENNA I like Pop Century resort. It's like taking a walk through the latter twentieth century and through Disney history. It's also a great value for budget-minded travelers—basic but very comfortable rooms, a convenient food court, and all the benefits of staying on Disney property.

wacky display of typical morning radio crew hi-jinks at unusually high decibels. It was then that I learned that the rooms are a little less soundproof than I would have preferred.

Still, others I know count Pop Century as their favorite value hotel. While it certainly is a step down in terms of ritz from some of the higher-end hotels, it retains the same level of service. Guests can take advantage of the Disney transportation system, they can have purchases shipped to the hotel, and can enjoy Extra Magic Hours at one of the theme parks. Also, Pop Century has its own bus stop. If you opt for one of the other value level resorts—the All Star Sports, Music or Movies—you'll likely hop on your hotel's bus and then have to make stops at the other nearby hotels before heading on to your destination. This alone puts Pop Century above all other value level resorts.

Port Orleans French Quarter

The Basics: Storm shutters, spicy Cajun food, garishly colored décor, ornate wrought iron fixtures and a feeling of perpetual Mardi Gras recreates New Orleans' French Quarter in this moderate-level resort.

The shuttered windows and doors along the main thoroughfare recreate perfectly the feel of Bourbon Street, as do the street signs, which are identical to those found in New Orleans.

The French Quarter boasts one of the more eye-popping pools, Doubloon Lagoon, which is themed like a Mardi Gras celebration. A large dragon twisting around one end also serves as a water slide, while an all-alligator Dixieland band stands guard nearby. Doubloon Lagoon is regularly rated as one of the top-themed pools at Walt Disney World. *(Rack rates range from $149 to $240 a night.)*

The Real Deal: I've been to New Orleans' French Quarter, and this resort does a remarkable job of recreating its look and feel. The background music, which is always there, makes it seem like, well, the real deal.

But, as it usually does, it all comes down to the food. Beignets and café au lait, ribs and cornbread make this a food court you will not want to overlook. And that, in itself, might be reason enough to stay at this resort.

Port Orleans Riverside

The Basics: Themed to resemble the old south, Port Orleans Riverside offers two types of rooms: Magnolia Bend (ornate southern mansion-style buildings) and Alligator Bend (rustic lodges.)

This resort is home to Boatwright's Dining Hall—a restaurant Mousejunkies Randy and Carol go out of their way to visit on many trips.

"It has a great breakfast," Randy opines. "The banana stuffed French toast is fantastic. Even if you're not staying there, and if you have a car, it's worth the drive." *(Rack rates at this moderate-level resort range from $149 to $240 a night.)*

The Real Deal: I will forever obstinately refer to this resort as Dixie Landings—which is what it was called when we stayed there.

It was the first trip back to Disney World since I fell into my addiction a year earlier. I could scarcely believe we were returning, and as we walked in to the airy, bright lobby, I could tell we had moved a step up, in terms of lodging, from our earlier trip. Accordion and washboard music lilted teasingly from behind bushes as we walked to our room in Magnolia Bend. We crossed a bridge spanning the Sassagoula River, which winds through the resort, and found our home for the next several days.

The rooms were bigger, had nicer furnishing, and even somehow smelled better. If it wasn't for the ribs at the French Quarter's food court, Riverside would top my list of moderate resorts.

Never underestimate the power of barbecue.

Caribbean Beach Resort

The Basics: A forty-five-acre lake, Barefoot Bay, sits at the center of this Caribbean-themed tropical resort. Cheerfully colorful buildings, immaculate grounds, and a location convenient to Epcot, Disney's Hollywood Studios, and Downtown Disney make this a great choice among moderate-level resorts.

Old Port Royale, located on the shores of Barefoot Bay, offers a food court, a table-service restaurant, shopping, an arcade, and bicycle and boat rentals.

This 200-acre resort is split up into five "island villages." Each of the thirty-three two-story buildings is divided into one of the island villages. The distance from Old Port Royale or the Custom House—the resort lobby—can be quite long. Request a room in Trinidad North or Martinique for a shorter walk to activities and the Spanish fort-themed pool at Old Port Royale. *(Rack rates at this moderate-level resort range from $149 to $240 a night.)*

The Real Deal: This place is huge. There are nine pools and five bus stops within the grounds of the Caribbean Beach Resort. Despite its size, the walk to your bus stop is likely to be rather short since there are so many of them.

The trek to the food court for breakfast could be another story. It's not unheard of to catch a bus just to get your morning pancakes before heading out to the theme parks for the day.

TIP *Visit the shores of Barefoot Bay near Old Port Royale each night at 9 P.M. for a distant, yet passable view of the Illuminations fireworks display at Epcot.*

The Yacht Club/Beach Club
The Basics: Sister resorts that sit on the shores of Crescent Lake, the Yacht Club and the Beach Club both reflect a New England oceanfront theme.

The Yacht Club aims to recreate a Martha's Vineyard/ Nantucket atmosphere from the late 1800s, while the Beach Club is themed to resemble a Cape Cod-style resort.

Location is key for these resorts, offering quick access to Epcot's International Gateway and Disney's Hollywood Studios. For foodies, there is no better location. Restaurants in both hotels are top notch, and after a short walk guests can find themselves choosing from the dining options in Epcot's World Showcase, or just across Crescent Lake at the Boardwalk Resort.

The amenities are elegant yet comfortable, and the resorts boast the best hotel pool on Disney property. Stormalong Bay features three acres of play area—shallow areas, sand-bottom pools, a whirlpool floating zone, and a striking "shipwreck" that houses an enclosed waterslide. *(Rooms at this deluxe resort range from $325 to $750, suites from $590 to $2,620.)*

The Real Deal: The pool is great. The lobbies are beautiful. The rooms are luxurious and the location is unmatched.

But it's all about the ice cream.

Beaches and Cream—an ice cream/burger joint located between the Yacht and Beach Club resorts—is reason enough to shell out the extra money these hotels charge. (A little hyperbole is acceptable when we're talking ice cream.) There's a $22 concoction called The Kitchen Sink, which features a vast amount of ice cream and toppings. It's the only

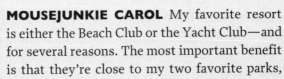

MOUSEJUNKIE CAROL My favorite resort is either the Beach Club or the Yacht Club—and for several reasons. The most important benefit is that they're close to my two favorite parks, Epcot and Disney's Hollywood Studios. Both resorts are within walking distance of these theme parks (if you have enough energy to do so) and—if you are so moved—both offer easier access to a wider variety of adult beverages.

This is key during the Halloween season when Epcot hosts the annual Food and Wine Festival. It's always nice to be right in the middle of the action, especially when it involves food and wine. These two sister resorts also share what is arguably the best pool on-site. The water-slide, the lazy river, and the sandy beach are unmatched anywhere on Disney property. It is also home to one of the very few character dining experiences that I will do. The Cape May Breakfast Buffet has a great variety of breakfast treats that I find wonderful. To be honest, the fact that they have characters, from my point-of-view, is a knock against them. But they know not to disturb a girl on the hunt for the breakfast pizza. (Which I highly recommend.)

ice cream-related dessert I've never been able to finish—a defeat I vow to one day avenge.

It's not so much the quality of the ice cream that makes The Kitchen Sink so great. (It's good, but I hail from Ben and Jerry's country.) It's the pageantry surrounding the challenge that makes it so much fun. Once it's constructed, a process that, in addition to ice cream, involves angel food cake, brownies, massive pillows of whipped cream and marshmallow and any number of toppings, it is delivered with great aplomb. An announcement is made and the restaurant lights are dimmed as it is hauled to the table.

My attempt at demolishing the Kitchen Sink included fellow Mousejunkies J, Walt, and Deb. We were ultimately unsuccessful, I believe, because Walt was playing injured (sprained esophagus). When it arrived with all the theatrical flair due such a majestic work of art, we attacked. There was little talking in the first few minutes, until J alerted us that he had found a vein of chocolate deep inside a mint chocolate chip cavern.

Not long after, Deb dropped out. However, that was to be expected. She is petite and did not claim to possess the ability to put away great volumes of food. Walt limped along while J and I returned to the trough, again and again. Eventually we admitted defeat, however. The grayish brown soup collecting at the bottom of the sink-shaped container mocked us.

Luckily, I was staying at the Beach Club, which meant I only had to waddle a short distance before falling face-first into my room and wondering whether I regretted such a foolhardy attempt. (For the record, I do not regret it. But this answer comes with the luxury of time and distance.)

Disney's Boardwalk Resort

The Basics: Designed to capture the look and feel of a 1920s-era Atlantic seaside resort, this deluxe-level hotel offers a nice range of dining and entertainment options. Its location, tucked into one corner of Crescent Lake, makes it incredibly convenient to both Epcot and Disney's Hollywood Studios.

The resort's themed pool, Luna Park, features a fantastic water slide—the Keister Coaster—and there are two quiet pools.

The Boardwalk Resort is within walking distance of several restaurants: The ESPN Club, the Boardwalk Bakery, Spoodles, Flying Fish Café, and the Big River Grille.

When the sun goes down, the resort comes alive. Entertainers work from one end of the boardwalk to the other, offering music, juggling, magic, and comedy shows. *(Room rates range from $325 to $790 a night, and suites range from $610 to $2,640.)*

The Real Deal: The Boardwalk is home. Having been lucky enough to stay there several times, it feels familiar and welcoming. The lobby's oversized chairs are perfect for my oversized back porch.

Its proximity to the ESPN Club, and that establishment's chicken wing and football-fueled Sundays, is yet another reason this place will forever feel like my home away from home.

There was a time when Amy and I walked through the Boardwalk Resort on our way somewhere. We were staying at a value-level resort at the time, and I remember looking up at the impossibly ornate carousel-horse chandelier in the hotel's entrance and saying, "We will never be able to stay here."

I had visions of oil billionaires and internet *wunderkinds* rubbing elbows and having a chuckle at us value resort

MOUSEJUNKIE WALT My favorite hotel is the Boardwalk, and the location is a big reason why. It's between my two favorite theme parks—Epcot and Disney's Hollywood Studios. And then there's the atmosphere. During the day it's a beautiful place to relax. At night there's entertainment from one end of the boardwalk to the other. There are jugglers, games of chance, musicians—all of which draw a crowd.

I also like the fact that it's its own little resort. There are restaurants, a piano bar, and a microbrewery there.

Think of it this way: If you went on a vacation there and didn't want to ride any of the attractions, you could just hang out at the Boardwalk Resort, maybe go to the pool and relax during the day. At night you can choose from any of the restaurants nearby, or walk right next door to Epcot and enjoy a different country every night. One night you could be drinking wine in Italy. The next you can be enjoying great French cuisine. If you want a trip where you just relax, it's the perfect place to do it.

Or you can go to the Magic Kingdom and be with all the screaming kids. Whatever floats your boat.

people. But as I accumulated more trips and experience—not to mention a few press events—I found that while the Boardwalk is pricey, there are ways to go about staying there without going flat broke.

Staying at the Boardwalk for the first half of January will get you a room for $335 a night. Is it a bargain? Only if you compare it to paying $530 a night for the same room just two weeks earlier. Also, Annual Passholders and AAA members can sometimes get a better rate, and occasionally room "codes" become available, saving even more money. Sites like mousesavers.com provide up-to-date deals. These rates are limited and may necessitate flexibility when picking dates.

The best way to save money at a resort like the Boardwalk is to rent Disney Vacation Club points. For an outline on how to rent points, see Chapter 10: Mousejunkies Marry.

Animal Kingdom Lodge

The Basics: This deluxe-level resort is themed to convey the feeling of being in an African wildlife reserve. The architecture, plant life, and variety of animals that roam large savannahs just outside the lobby contribute to a vivid and convincing atmosphere.

Guests can get an up-close look at the animals from a viewing area—Arusha Rock—located outside the main lobby, or from their rooms if they have interior-facing accommodations.

Opened in 2001, this resort has two table-service restaurants, a counter-service restaurant, and two bars—Uzima Springs and Victoria Falls.

Concierge-level guests are offered a safari experience unique to resort guests: The Sunset, or Wanyama, safari. It runs roughly ninety minutes and takes guests on a recreation of an African game drive across the resort's savannahs. The safaris conclude with a multi-course meal at the hotel's premier restaurant, Jiko.

Disney's Animal Kingdom Lodge was named "Best Theme Park Hotel" for 2008 by Theme Park Insider. The award was given for the highest average reader reviews over the twelve-month period ending May 31, 2008. Animal Kingdom Lodge previously won this award in 2005 and 2006. *(Room rates range from $225 to $675 a night, with suites running from $705 to $2,840 nightly. This resort is also a Disney Vacation Club resort.)*

The Real Deal: The persistent image of this resort pushed by Disney public relations is that of a guest sitting out on a hotel room balcony in the morning, sipping coffee, as a giraffe slowly moves by, grazing on leaves just a few feet away.

In reality, that is exactly what it's like to stay at the Animal Kingdom Lodge (assuming you score a savanna-view room.) There's no marketing ploy at work here. It is as beautiful and unique an experience as you'll find without actually traveling to Africa.

More than three hundred animals and birds populate the grounds, which surround the resort on three sides. The animals can be seen from private balconies as well as several public viewing areas.

There's nothing like sharing a caffeine buzz with a zebra first thing in the morning.

The Contemporary Resort

The Basics: Built in conjunction with the Magic Kingdom, the Contemporary Resort is one of the original two Walt

Disney World hotels. Constructed in a modular style and then pieced together on-site, its location is one of its biggest draws. Sitting between the Seven Seas Lagoon and Bay Lake, the resort affords guests an unmatched view of the Magic Kingdom theme park.

Monorails glide quietly right through the center of the hotel, stopping in the Grand Canyon Concourse to whisk visitors off and return them to one of several restaurants and recreation options available nearby. *(Rack rates for standard rooms range from $270 to $795 a night. Suites range from $885 to $2,340 a night, while the vice presidential and presidential suites approach $3,000 a night.)*

The Real Deal: The Contemporary is a pricey but incredibly convenient option for guests intending to spend the bulk of their time at the Magic Kingdom. The key element here is location. Assuming you're in the tower, you step out of your room and on to the monorail, which gets to the Magic Kingdom in seconds and to Epcot after a transfer at the Ticket and Transportation Center. It cuts down on time spent on the bus, and ensures you remain blanketed by the magic.

Until recently, however, it still boasted the woefully dated original style and décor. This means the rooms resembled the back seat of a 1976 AMC Pacer. Loud, dissonant colors and patterns created a look that conjured images of spilling a warm Fresca on someone's pantsuit. It gave me a headache and charged me a lot of money for the pleasure.

Luckily, that has changed. A rehab several years ago has brought the rooms up-to-date. Flat-screen TVs, computers with internet access, and darker, muted colors combine to make the Contemporary worth its price tag, if you have the means.

I didn't exactly have the means, but a collision of circumstances found us ensconced in this hotel for one night in December of 2006. We were in the Garden Wing, which is a short walk from the main building. The view from the back of the hotel, where we stayed, was striking: as we walked from our room to the lobby one morning, the sun was just poking up over the trees at Fort Wilderness. The deep orange hues painted Bay Lake brilliantly as the rays warmed the early winter morning. It was an unexpected wake-up call, and in some ways it may have exceeded the iconic view of Cinderella Castle available to those with a room on the front of the Tower Wing.

Old Key West

The Basics: The first Disney Vacation Club resort built, this resort offers the laid-back charms of Key West with the service and amenities Disney resorts are known for.

Guests can use DVC points or book through central reservations. Villas are offered in four configurations: Studio, one-bedroom, two-bedroom and three-bedroom Grand Villas. The rooms at Old Key West are quite large, culminating in the absolutely gargantuan 2,375-square-foot Grand Villa.

Guests can dine at Olivia's or get something quick at Good's Food To-Go. Old Key West offers guests volleyball, shuffleboard, basketball, golf, and tennis courts. There are four swimming pools, playgrounds, and a fitness center for those who may have suffered from the aforementioned head trauma and think exercising on vacation is a good idea.

Guests can also travel to Downtown Disney by boat, which is a much more enjoyable option than the typical bus trip. *(Old Key West is a Disney Vacation Club Resort, but guests can book through central reservations. Room rates start at a studio—$285 to $410, and top out at the Grand Villa, which runs from $1,170 to $1,645 a night.)*

The Real Deal: I swore up and down that I wouldn't like Old Key West. All I heard was that it was the oldest of the DVC resorts and wasn't necessarily convenient to any particular park.

I could not have been more wrong.

Old Key West is now among my preferred resorts. The rooms are large, sure, but it's really the laid-back feel of the place. After dark the resort comes alive with festive yet muted lighting, rather successfully recreating the feel of the original location several hundred miles to the south.

We gathered with most of the Mousejunkies one night at the Gurgling Suitcase bar, located on the dock at the Sassagoula River. I happened to be wearing a large button announcing to anyone who walked by that it was my birthday. I stepped up to the bar, ordered several drinks and waited. The bartender came back and asked, "Is it really your birthday?" I said it was, and she comped the drinks.

If there's one way to a journalist's heart, it's through his liver.

Fort Wilderness

MOUSEJUNKIE JENNA My favorite non-DVC resort would have to be Fort Wilderness Resort and Campground. You want to talk recreation? The Fort has volleyball, basketball and tennis courts, shuffleboard, horseshoes, fishing, a marina, nightly wagon rides, a dog park (pets are welcome in certain camping loops), is adjacent to the petting farm and riding stables, has a great view of the Electrical Water Pageant, is home to both a dinner show and a character meal, and some of the best resort transportation I've ever experienced.

And it has the topper—Chip n' Dales Campfire Sing-Along, a free forty-minute outdoor show featuring songs, jokes, and Chip and Dale. You can bring your own marshmallows or s'mores, or buy them there. Afterward, you can stick around for a Disney feature shown on the big movie screen. It's kind of like going to camp and the drive-in all in one night. The Campfire Sing-Along is open and free to all Disney guests, so if the campground atmosphere doesn't appeal, you can still enjoy the show. I have not stayed in the cabins, but I found the RV sites and comfort stations top-notch. *(Campsite rates range from $42 to $111 and cabin rates range from $255 to $395.)*

Saratoga Springs

The Basics: The spirit of Saratoga Springs, New York, with its horse racing history and placid upstate feel, is recreated accurately in the fifth Disney Vacation Club resort.

Victorian architecture and gurgling springs evoke a gentler age. Overstuffed chairs make the lobby a comfortable place to meet friends, and its spa offers a relaxing way to get away from the theme parks. *(This is a Disney Vacation Club resort, but accommodations, which range from studio rooms to three-bedroom grand villas, range from $285 to $1,645 a night.)*

The Real Deal: This resort is gargantuan. Plan on packing a lunch if you want to walk to the check-in desk from the one of the more far-flung buildings. The complex was built in three phases, making it the largest of all DVC properties.

It was constructed on the site of the old Disney Institute, so guests can walk to Downtown Disney, or take a quick ferry across the lake. Rooms facing Downtown Disney have a fantastic view of the nearly twenty-four-hour restaurant, shopping, and nightclub district.

TIP *For a room closest to the check-in desk, request The Springs. For a room closest to Downtown Disney, request a room in Congress Park.*

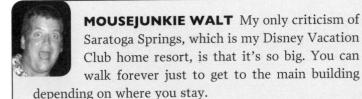

MOUSEJUNKIE WALT My only criticism of Saratoga Springs, which is my Disney Vacation Club home resort, is that it's so big. You can walk forever just to get to the main building depending on where you stay.

MOUSEJUNKIE JENNA If money was no object, these are my top five "Can this be my room? Please?" rooms at Walt Disney World: The King Kamehameha Suite at the Polynesian; the Steeplechase Suite at the Boardwalk; the Newport Suite at the Beach Club; the Yellowstone Suite at the Wilderness Lodge; and the Royal Assante Suite at the Animal Kingdom Lodge.

You really want to get your Disney trip craving wheels turning at warp speed? Visit this web site: www.suitedisney.com/wdwphotos/suites/index.htm. Of course, the least any of those rooms cost is $910 per night (Yellowstone in Value season), and they go up to $2,840 per night (Royal Assante in Holiday season), so that's one Disney Dream that may well go unfulfilled.

Mousejunkies Eat

Get This Man to a Buffet!

DON'T FOOL YOURSELF INTO THINKING of eating at Disney World as a secondary experience. As a fellow Mousejunkie once noted: "Disney is all about the food."

The sheer number of restaurant choices is staggering, and can range from pretty standard to extraordinary. After more than twenty trips to Walt Disney World and countless meals, I've really only begun to scratch the surface.

TIP *Make your reservations as early as possible, or plan on standing in line at counter service during your stay. Advanced Dining Reservations (ADRs) can be made 90 days out from your trip by calling (407) WDW-DINE (939-3463).*

When traveling to Walt Disney World, planning where and when to eat is of the utmost importance. In fact, our entire trip is usually planned around where we want to eat. While it may sound crazy, believe this: if you don't plan far enough ahead you'll be munching on churros and turkey legs or standing in line for a burger the whole time. Trust me, I not only love Disney World, I love to eat. Have you *seen* my photo in "About the Author"?

There are many ways to attack a dining plan—from what to eat to how to pay for it (and pay you will).

Before we dive headfirst into one of my favorite Disney World topics, gird your loins and prepare for sticker shock. Dining on-property is expensive no matter how you go about it. And before we start in earnest let me provide this initial tip: Don't be the guy who wants to save money by packing peanut butter sandwiches and juice boxes for the afternoon. Don't be that guy. We see that family and we weep. Eating great food is one of the most fun, satisfying things in life. Leave the cooler at home and dive headlong into Lake Debt with me.

The Mousejunkies as a group savor Disney dining with a unique gusto. Take, for example, this e-mail I received from Mousejunkie J just days before a group of us were to meet up for a week at Disney's Boardwalk Resort. J is healthy, runs every day, and is a lot smarter than I am. He set the bar with this missive:

> *"I just had a real donut. I am weaning off the diet in order to prep myself for the carnage to come. I need to stretch out my stomach so I can take full advantage of the buffets."*

It wasn't long before this prompted a follow up e-mail from Adam, a fellow traveler who would be joining us:

> *"We'll need to figure out a buddy system for when one of us eats 'past the limit' and can't physically walk themselves out of a restaurant. Friends don't let friends walk engorged."*

That's right, a "buddy system" for a buffet. That's why I travel with these people.

Both J and Adam are veterans of the Disney buffet campaigns. "Buffet," a French word meaning, "I'll have more," is a term often used when planning to eat at Disney World. There are a number of buffets scattered throughout the parks and resorts, some better than others.

Travel experts may tell you that a buffet is a waste of a Disney Dining Plan credit (a way of pre-paying for the meal). I say it's a method of delivering more food to my gullet efficiently—value be damned.

Let's say, hypothetically, you had a three-year-old daughter and you chose not to bring her along on a particular trip. She really couldn't take "Disney is not for children" as an excuse, so you're fairly wracked with guilt. What else can a vacationer do but drown his or her sorrows in the warm and welcoming embrace of the buffet?

Buffets are the great equalizer. They are the melting pot of vacations. It's there you'll find the best and worst of humanity—patient, gracious people eating elbow-to-elbow with wild-eyed, raving lunatics who will mow down a three-year-old if the tyke stands between them and the carving station.

That said, let's tour what I consider the best buffets of Walt Disney World.

Buffets

The Crystal Palace

The Basics: Located at the end of Main Street USA in the Magic Kingdom this buffet is always reliable and has great food. The Crystal Palace is also a character meal, which means Disney characters—in this case Winnie the Pooh, Tigger, Eeyore and Piglet—come around to each table and interact with diners. That's nice, but for his own sake please keep Eeyore out of my way when I've got the breakfast lasagna (waffles, pound cake, fruit and custard topped with pastry cream) in my sights. *COST: $18.99 (breakfast) to $27.99 (dinner) for adults, $10.99 to $12.99 Children ages 3-9.*

The Real Deal: I was in line at the Crystal Palace buffet one morning when a youngster in front of me started stacking bacon on his plate. The kid was probably ten or eleven—certainly old enough to know better. He just kept grabbing handfuls of bacon, laughing, and stacking it on his plate. When he was satisfied he had enough—his plate looked like he was playing pork Tetris—he turned to walk away and dropped the plate on the floor. He stood looking at the pile of broken glass and meat for a second, shrugged his shoulders and then ran off. At that moment I started to understand why dining at a theme park costs so much.

At another meal at the Crystal Palace I inadvertently became that which I loathe most: The Stupid Guest. At the outset of this missive, let me just state that when it comes to math, I am a complete idiot. We were using a combination of the pre-paid Disney Dining Plan and cash. On top of that I was suffering from a winter cold and was flying pretty high on cold medicine. At the end of the meal the waiter brought over the bill. I handled it, dividing the cost up between our large group and figuring out the tip. The cast member came and took it away.

A minute later he returned and handed it back to me. He sheepishly told me that I was short about $10. I apologized profusely, added some money and he went away.

Another minute passed and the waiter came back and informed me again that I was short cash. Dumbfounded, I saw the look on his face and I read it thusly: "These cheap jerks are trying to screw me out of some money."

Pretty sure that this kid had to deal with such a situation on a fairly regular basis, I was mortified. At this point I was also confused, so I threw a handful of cash into the pile and apologized profusely. I've seen, firsthand, how thoughtless and downright mean guests can be to cast members, and I swore I'd always go out of my way to make sure I never behaved in a similar fashion. I'd always done my best, but I can say with a fair amount of certainty that he didn't buy my plea of ignorance for a second. To him I'm sure I came off as a typical rude tourist determined to get out of there spending as little as possible.

Yet, as I've seen scores of times, he was professional, patient, and incredibly gracious. He told me he was sorry he had to ask me for more money, and was embarrassed to have to inconvenience me. Which made me feel even worse.

The cast members at the Crystal Palace are unfailingly cheerful, attentive, and fun. Even when pushed to the limit.

Perhaps the most important benefit of dining at the Crystal Palace—and the importance of this cannot be understated—is that this restaurant has the strongest air conditioning of any restaurant on Disney property. On the Mousejunkie "Save Me From Heat Stroke" scale, the Crystal Palace ranks a 10. It is the standard against which all other eateries are measured. Within seconds of finding sanctuary in its glass-encased walls and navigating the brightly lit dining room, you'll sit down, cool down, and chow down. No matter what time of year you're patronizing the place, you'll be shivering by the time you leave.

Crystal Palace air conditioning supervisor—I salute you.

Boma

The Basics: Located in the Animal Kingdom Lodge, Boma boasts "flavors of Africa."

That may be true, but I know prime rib and chicken fingers when I see them. Don't get me wrong, the food at Boma is great—it's just not as exotic as advertised. There are a few items you don't normally find around the house, (Pap and Fufu—which I mention only because they're fun to say) but overall it's a fairly familiar experience. *COST: $16.99 (breakfast) to $26.99(dinner) for adults, $9.99 to $12.99 for children 3-9.*

The Real Deal: I'm a huge fan of the prime rib—Bomanians will refer to it as "wood-roasted meats"—if only because they provide a number of different sauces to go along with it. And I'm a sauce guy. Additionally, the peanut rice is worth the price of admission alone. Ask Mousejunkie Carol, however, and she'll wax poetic about the zebra dome desserts.

No matter which end of the buffet line you start at, there's something for everyone at Boma. And while some of it may stray toward African-themed cuisine, you won't find poached wildebeast on the menu.

I've long railed against giving up little-known facts on Disney forums and message boards, only because it creates an entitlement class. Mention a special moment on a forum and soon hordes of sweaty vacationers are demanding it daily. Eventually, because of the demands of such guests, the experience in question is retired. For example:

At dinner one night our group of ten was surprised by Boma chef Tjet Jep, who came to our table personally with a bowl in his hands. With great ceremony and flourish he announced he had made a special dessert for our table. We were to use our hands to eat, and we were not to use the linen napkins in front of us to clean up.

"The cleaning bills are too expensive," he laughed.

With that, he placed the bowl on the table without giving us a hint as to what was inside. We all hesitantly prodded the light-brown, deep fried, chocolate-drizzled pods stacked in it.

Only Mousejunkie Randy smiled knowingly.

One of our group finally overcame any initial trepidation, grabbed one and tossed it down. Tjet Jep had gifted us with two bowls of deep-fried Oreos—a perfect pile of steaming, gooey, fluffy, golden treats not available for purchase or even mentioned on the menu.

Mousejunkie Randy had worked his magic. When we arrived he spotted Tjet Jep, singled him out and lavished him with praise. Randy has a way with words, and his love of all things Disney, and specifically Boma, is evident. The result? A pile of the richest, sweetest treats I've ever tasted, all thanks to a kind chef.

Obviously we weren't the first group to enjoy this unexpected experience, and we weren't the last. (Actually, on two subsequent trips Randy worked his "Fried Oreo Gambit" successfully.) But it wasn't a common occurrence. Until a massive and well-known Disney forum got hold of the story. Before long, visitors were demanding special treatment and asking outright for JT's specialty. The fried Oreos have now been retired.

Still, Boma holds a few secrets.

TIP *Be nice to the Disney chefs. You never know how they will return a few kind words.*

Perhaps my most treasured brush with fame also occurred at the Animal Kingdom Lodge's wonderful buffet. One morning at breakfast, Carol, Randy, J and I sat bleary-eyed and awaiting our glasses of Frunch, Boma's unique and refreshing breakfast beverage. (Another reason to make plans there.)

Randy sat down across from me, did a small doubletake and asked, "Is that John Cleese?"

A lifelong Monty Python fan, I scoffed. Then I turned to look. Then I caught my breath. John Cleese—the Black Knight, Archie Leach, Basil Fawlty, the Minister of Silly Walks—sat down at a table not yards from where we were. His head topped with a large-brimmed straw hat, his face was unmistakable. He talked with his wife, daughter, and a Disney guide as we openly gawked for a few seconds.

I passed my camera across the table and asked Randy to pretend to take a picture of me, but really focus the camera on the comic legend just over my shoulder. All through breakfast we stole glances, not wishing to bother him but not wanting to look away, either.

We finished up and gathered near the restrooms while we waited for one of our party to freshen up. Cleese walked by us and went into the men's room. When he was inside we began to gush anew, breaking into Silly Walks and some of our worst Python voices. When he emerged he walked by our group and over to his wife—who was standing behind us the whole time. She saw every Silly Walk, heard every Mrs. Creosote impression we could muster.

My advice? Eat at Boma. Maybe you'll see John Cleese. I did.

While there are many other buffet and family-style restaurants, the king of them all is 'Ohana.

'Ohana

The Basics: Located in the Polynesian Resort, 'Ohana offers Hawaiian-style dining, entertainment, and a fantastic view of the Magic Kingdom across the Seven Seas Lagoon. *COST: $18.99 (breakfast) to $26.99 (dinner) for adults, $10.99 to $12.99 for children 3-9.*

The Real Deal: While not technically a buffet, food is served family style, which to me means "eat it, they'll bring more."

One of my favorite Disney World traditions, and something I've been lucky enough to do on more than a few occasions, goes like this: Arrive early and claim a seat on the corner of the bar just outside the restaurant. Order two

'Ohana Coladas (because two will get you very, very comfortable), turn the seat to the right so it faces the large window overlooking the resort, and watch the sky catch fire over the lake.

The central Florida sunset offers those lucky enough with a front row view a vivid display. The atmosphere is painted a brilliant orange with highlights of red and blue flecking the edges. And there is no better vantage point than looking out across the Seven Seas Lagoon from the Polynesian Resort.

TIP _Arrive for dinner early. The bar outside the restaurant is the most welcoming and relaxing on-property. At night, guests can enjoy entertainment provided by a musician strumming an acoustic guitar and crooning Hawaiian favorites, while the centrally-located fountain in the lobby below provides a natural and relaxing backing track._

Some will tell you that _'Ohana_ means "family." In reality, _'Ohana_ is the Polynesian word for "I ate so much I think I'm going to puke." Because that's how I've felt every single time I've eaten at this restaurant. The food is too good and too plentiful.

Within minutes of being seated, your server begins piling the food in front of you. It all starts with pork dumplings, honey-coriander chicken wings, scalloped potatoes, and stir-fried vegetables (which are more for decoration than eating, as far as I'm concerned, primarily because they're not made of beef). Just when you think you're stuffed to the point of bursting, the meat arrives. Servers scurry from one side of the restaurant to the other, delivering skewers of seared pork loin, sirloin steak, and mesquite turkey, all of which are grilled over an open oak fire pit.

It's tempting to gorge on whatever meat arrives first. My advice, however, is to graze until the turkey arrives—at which point you can unleash the appetite. The mesquite-grilled turkey, dipped in peanut sauce, is juicy, tender, and savory.

It is the kind of meal that inspires poets, songwriters, and fat guys. Many's the cold New England winter night I've dreamt of those coriander chicken wings as a ukulele strums liltingly in the background.

A cast member serenades guests with Hawaiian songs. Children can take part in a limbo contest and coconut shell races are held several times throughout the night.

I've been able to spend several evenings looking across the lagoon at Cinderella Castle as brilliant fireworks hurtle through the air all around it. If your reservations are earlier than the nightly "Wishes" fireworks display, finish up your meal and waddle uncomfortably down to the beach. Stake out a spot in the sand—or if you're extremely lucky, sack out in a hammock—and enjoy the show from there. After "Wishes" you'll have a front-row seat for the Electrical Water Pageant. The waterborne parade floats across the Seven Seas Lagoon and Bay Lake nightly, weather permitting.

Buffets and family-style restaurants are plentiful throughout Disney property. Here's a list of restaurants where you can eat until you commit at least three of the Seven Deadly Sins:

➤ **Epcot:** Akershus Royal Banquet Hall (not strictly a buffet, but it is all-you-can-eat), Biergarten Restaurant, Garden Grill (all-you-can-eat).

➤ **Disney's Hollywood Studios:** Hollywood & Vine.

➤ **Magic Kingdom:** Crystal Palace, Liberty Tree Tavern (family style), Cinderella's Royal Table (family style for breakfast only, normal menu throughout the day).

➤ **Resorts:** 1900 Park Faire (Grand Floridian Resort), Boma (Animal Kingdom Lodge), Cape May Buffet (Beach Club Resort), Chef Mickey's (Contemporary Resort), 'Ohana (Polynesian Resort), Trail's End Buffeteria (Fort Wilderness).

TIP *Watch the nightly "Wishes" fireworks display and the Electrical Water Pageant from the beach at the Polynesian. The music accompanying each show is piped-in, and there's plenty of room to spread out and even lie down.*

Meals with Character

If you're going to Walt Disney World with kids, you'll want to squeeze in a character meal or two. I'd recommend two. **The Crystal Palace,** in the Magic Kingdom, where you'll find Winnie the Pooh and friends, and **Chef Mickey's** at the Contemporary Resort, where you'll find Mickey, Minnie, Goofy, Pluto and Donald Duck. The food at these restaurants ranges from quite good to passable.

Chef Mickey's, in particular, leaves me conflicted. It's boisterous, fun, and has a great view of the Magic Kingdom. At the same time, the food is mediocre at best.

And while it's fun to swing linen napkins around over your head (which is part of the dinner show). I get uncomfortable with the thought of half-chewed food flying through the air after being launched from one of the celebratory linens. Also, I've seen more kids sifting through the food with their bare hands and then putting it back at Chef Mickey's than at any other buffet on-property. I'm not naïve enough to think it doesn't happen elsewhere, I just don't want to know or think about it.

When we brought our three-year-old daughter, we went to a few character meals. It was fun the first time, fun the second time, but then it got to be "how many of these character meals do we really need?" They're fun, but two will suffice.

TIP *Book character meals, but don't feel like you've got to hit them all. They start to feel a bit repetitive by about the 890th photo-op.*

That said, there are also the character meals at **Cinderella's Royal Table** located in Cinderella Castle in the Magic Kingdom, and **Akershus Royal Banquet Hall** in the Norway pavilion at Epcot. Both are princess meals—which means if you have a young daughter it's the be-all, end-all of character meals. That being the case, you may have very likely guessed that it's not an easy reservation to get. If you haven't called 90 days out (or 100 days out if you're staying on-property), right at 7 A.M. with a huge amount of luck, you're very likely not going to get in. Dial quickly, because the princesses visit Norway for breakfast only. The rest of the day you can expect normal Norwegian fare—fish, served primarily by tall, blond, statuesque cast members.

I approach it like this: Norway is a good substitute if you can't get into Cinderella's Royal Table.

Character meals can be found at these restaurants:

- ➤ 1900 Park Faire
- ➤ Akershus Royal Banquet Hall (breakfast)
- ➤ Cape May Café (breakfast)
- ➤ Chef Mickey's
- ➤ Cinderella's Royal Table
- ➤ Crystal Palace
- ➤ Garden Grill Restaurant
- ➤ Garden Grove Café
- ➤ Hollywood and Vine
- ➤ Liberty Tree Tavern
- ➤ Mickey's Backyard Barbecue
- ➤ 'Ohana (breakfast)
- ➤ Tusker House (breakfast)

Can't Miss Restaurants

Epcot

If you can get into **Le Cellier**, in the Canada pavilion, do so. It's popular, so it can be difficult to get a reservation. If you expect to walk up and be seated, I mock you. Don't miss the cheddar cheese soup with breadsticks.

It's food and entertainment. It's beer and sausages and an oompah band adding a healthy dose of atmosphere.

MOUSEJUNKIE WALT: My favorite restaurant is **Le Cellier** in the Canada pavilion at Epcot. I'm a steak guy anyway, but I love the pretzel breadsticks and the cheddar-and-bacon beer soup. I'm French Canadian, so I feel like these are my people. The cast members there are among the friendliest anywhere, and are more than happy to talk about their home provinces. The beer is good, the bread is good, and the atmosphere is good. There's nothing not to like about Le Cellier.

Other than that, I can only advise to call as far ahead as you can to make advanced dining reservations. This is necessary even in non-peak seasons because of the Disney Dining Plan (an option where guests can pre-pay a flat rate for their meals.) If you don't make reservations ahead of time and you think you're going to get down there and walk into a restaurant and be seated, you are mistaken.

It's the **Biergarten** in the Germany pavilion. The food is mainly pork, potato, and sausage-related, but you can wash it all down while swinging a frothy tankard back and forth. And I've found the more beer you have, the more fun the Biergarten gets.

Nearby: You can walk out the International Entrance near the UK pavilion to get to the Boardwalk. It's worth the walk, especially at night. And you can eat at **The ESPN Club**. The food is good, and the atmosphere is a lot of fun—especially if your home team is playing a game.

In fact, there may be no more fun place to spend a Sunday afternoon, than at the ESPN Club at the Boardwalk Resort. To take advantage of the place most efficiently in the fall requires planning.

A Sunday during football season when your favorite NFL team is playing at 1 P.M. calls for only one thing: an all-day chicken wing and beer orgy. And there is no more comfortable place to conduct this activity than the back corner booth at the ESPN Club—of which there is approximately one.

The trick is to arrive early. There are two sides to the restaurant—the bar side and the restaurant side. The booths are located on the bar side, and there are only seven of those. The ESPN Club opens at 11:30 A.M. on game day. Plan on arriving by 10 A.M. at the latest if you plan to claim a booth. There will be others in line, and it's not unheard of for fans of the Washington Redskins to form an unholy alliance with Dallas Cowboy fans so they all can secure their favorite seating.

Get in the right-hand line. When the doors open, it's everyone for themselves. Run to the right and head for the back. Every booth has its own TV, which can be changed to whatever game you'd like to watch. There is one large screen that will show a game with audio—something decided by a show of hands once the bar is full.

The word from the game day host cast members is this: if there is a New England Patriots Game or a Philadelphia Eagles game, it will more likely than not end up on the big screen. These two teams seem to draw the most fans on game day.

Counter service at Epcot is fairly standard, with the standout being **Cantina de San Angel**. The offerings are a little different, and you can sit right on the water while you eat.

Disney's Hollywood Studios

The **'50s Prime Time Café** is fun—but you have to be in the mood to interact with cast members immersed in their roles. The theming—think American 1950s and 60s—and the cast are top-notch. The food, especially lunch, has been very mediocre. (Aside from the peanut butter-and-jelly shake, which is reason enough to book a flight to Orlando.) One of the best waiters in all of Walt Disney World, Loukili, a cast member from Morocco, works there. He's sarcastic, funny, and takes his time with guests to make sure they're having fun. Request him. Tip him well.

Mama Melrose's Ristorante Italiano offers delicious Italian fare, but more importantly it's one of the Fantasmic Dinner Package Restaurants. If you book a Fantasmic Dinner Package meal, you are seated at a specific time and presented with a pass that provides reserved seating at Disney Hollywood Studio's nightly Fantasmic show. (This helps guests avoid having to show up two hours early for a decent spot.) It doesn't cost extra, but the seating times are limited.

However, another one of Disney's finest cast members, a waiter named Kevin from Orlando, has been known to provide such passes to kind, patient guests whether they've booked the package or not. The only way to find out is to ask, and as always a kind word and patience can go a long

MOUSEJUNKIE JENNA Among my favorites is the **Hollywood Brown Derby** at Disney's Hollywood Studios. I have two reasons for liking it: First, the ambiance. When I step into the Derby, I instantly feel ten times more glamorous and refined—even when I'm sweaty and frazzled and decked out in shorts and an ice cream-stained t-shirt. The swank decor and caricatures make me feel like I might be some starlet out for a night on the town. Second: the food. The filet mignon is hands-down the best I have ever had. It's tender and flavorful and I can order it as rare as I want because they know how to do it perfectly. Precede that with a scallop or crab cake appetizer and the world seems pretty darned perfect.

Here's another vote for 'Ohana. I don't care how many times they change up the menu, they still offer huge amounts of tasty food and a great overall dining experience. And as long as the turkey, the sirloin and the bread pudding are on the menu, they can change whatever they want. Besides which, I love the giant flower/water feature chlorine/tiki god tropicalness of the Polynesian. It's festive without trying too hard.

way with the highly-motivated and skilled cast members at Walt Disney World.

Counter service at Disney's Hollywood Studios is incredibly standard. It doesn't matter where you choose to eat, it's pretty much the same fare you find at any counter service restaurant on Disney property offering burgers and such.

There is one notable exception: Do not eat at the **ABC Commissary**. The service can be unusually slow and the food is substandard. The burgers tasted boiled. The dessert was inedible. The Cuban sandwich, while notable by its departure from the ordinary, was dry and lacked anything approaching flavor. The place has a reputation for being among the least desirable counter-service choices, and we found reports of its nastiness to be accurate. Don't eat there. Just...don't. It would be better to trap one of those little lizards that are all over the place and then let it bake on the sidewalk and eat that.

Animal Kingdom

For food? Skip it. Nothing to see here. Just move along.

There is a **Rainforest Café** located at the entrance of the park, but it's run-of-the-mill, expensive, and really just Disney-lite. The newly-opened **Yak & Yeti Restaurant** is a welcome addition, but not reason enough to waste a reservation on. I'd suggest getting on a bus and shooting over to the Animal Kingdom Lodge and eating at **Boma**.

Elsewhere Around the World

Looking for a quiet, out of the way place to have a romantic dinner? Steer clear of the **Whispering Canyon Café** in the Wilderness Lodge. (If you go: Take a boat from the Magic Kingdom.) It is loud, brash, bright, and energetic.

TIP *Want to shake up the dining experience? Make sure to ask for ketchup at the Whispering Canyon Café. Every bottle* *from surrounding tables will suddenly be transported to your area by boisterous, mischievous servers.*

The Grand Sandwich at the **Grand Floridian Café** is a criminally well-kept secret. (If you go: Take the monorail from the Magic Kingdom to the Grand Floridian Resort. The restaurant is on the main floor just off the lobby.) The Grand Sandwich is an open-faced hot turkey, ham, bacon and tomato concoction—and here's the genius of it all—topped with a rich boursin cheese sauce and fried onion straws. I'm firmly convinced you can top anything with a rich boursin cheese sauce and fried onion straws and it'll be great. The Grand Floridian Café is often overlooked by guests in favor of the marquee eateries. These guests don't know what they're missing.

Downtown Disney

The best value on-property is **The Earl of Sandwich**. It's a sub/sandwich shop. But the sandwiches are great and the prices are actually cheap—which is rare on Disney property. It's so cheap, that people who work at Downtown Disney eat there—so it's always crowded.

For years I said the California Grill was my favorite restaurant in all of Walt Disney World, but I lied. That title may actually now go to **Raglan Road**, an Irish pub-themed restaurant located just off the Pleasure Island section of Downtown Disney. The food revolves around Irish themes, but is much better than anything I've sampled while actually in that section of the world. The Simple Salmon appetizer—smoked salmon served with capers, shallots and creme fraiche—is a highlight, along with Ger's Bread and Butter

Pudding. The music is fantastic, and the Irish step dancer, who performs nightly, is the best you'll find outside of the Emerald Isle.

TIP   *Schedule your dinner for after 8 P.M.—which is when the live entertainment begins at Raglan Road.*

Mousejunkies Splurge

There are good meals and bad meals at Walt Disney World. And then there are the transcendent.

Don't let anyone tell you the food at Walt Disney World is all about burgers and Mickey-shaped ice cream bars. Trust me, I've been to the **California Grill**, and I'd be hard pressed to name a better restaurant anywhere. I'd also be hard-pressed to even stand after a meal at this restaurant, because even though the portions are not huge, this is a dinner of many courses.

Yes, I do live in the land of chain restaurants. No, I don't worship at the altar of Applebees. Therefore, you must trust me when I say that the California Grill is a very impressive place to get some dinner. Perched atop the fifteenth floor of the Contemporary Resort, it is one of Disney's finest restaurants. The view is breathtaking and the Pacific Coast cuisine is prepared "on stage" by Disney's chefs.

According to cast members, securing a wait-staff position at the California Grill is a difficult and highly competitive process. Essentially, someone has to die for a position to open up. They are highly trained, knowledgeable, and efficient.

MOUSEJUNKIE J: My first Recommendation would be the **Kona Café** located in the Polynesian resort. I have eaten all three meals there and they were all excellent. It is laid back but the food is great. Dinner has great selections from a filet to mahi-mahi. It's not cheap, but it's reasonable by Disney standards. The fresh bread with the honey-macadamia nut butter is to die for. And let us not forget the best breakfast item in Walt Disney World—Tonga Toast. How can you go wrong deep frying anything and then rolling it in cinnamon sugar? I had a pulled pork sandwich there for lunch and it was very good.

My second recommendation has to be the **'50s Primetime Café** at Disney's Hollywood Studios. The place has a fantastic atmosphere and the fare is comfort food at its best—plus there is nothing over $20 on the menu. Just be prepared to 'play the game' with the servers. The pot roast with mashed potatoes is excellent. Just remember to ask for no green beans if you are not going to eat the green beans. Standing in the corner because you did not finish them is a drag. (Yes, seriously.) To top it off, the dessert menu is presented to diners on a ViewMaster. It's the perfect ending to a meal that takes guests back to their youth.

(Continued on next page)

On one particular visit, our waiter was able to describe our wine selection in such detail, he noted that the grapes were grown on the western side of an island that gets more wind, and therefore affects the grapes in a specific manner.

You'll very likely find the place to be crowded and loud—just the way it is intended to be. The Tune-In lounge before the meal is really neat as well. Just like you were transported back in time. Most importantly, they serve Yuengling Lager.

For a real nice meal that makes you feel like you are dining five-star but on a budget eat at **Les Chefs de France**—*for lunch*. It is a beautiful dining room, the service is very good and the lunch prices are a bargain by Disney standards. They serve fresh French rolls with butter that are mouth watering. The wine by the glass is reasonable as well. I always get the Bier Kronenbourg 1664. Despite the setting—white linen tablecloths and servers in white dress shirts with black ties—I still felt fine in a polo shirt and shorts. The flatbreads are excellent as well as the stuffed crepes. You can go more expensive and get a dinner-type meal at lunchtime.

Normally I would put **Le Cellier** on any list but it can by pricey if you get a drink and a filet mignon. The menu is really a steak menu with a single pasta and seafood choice. Don't get me wrong, I love the place. If I knew the people going had lots of disposable income, I would tell them to go there in an instant.

The only thing he left out was that the postman in the village where the grapes are grown drops packages outside the general store on alternating Wednesdays. This guy knew his stuff.

On this night, the first course consisted of a mushroom flatbread. I hate mushrooms, (and beans and olives—all of which are foods which only work for evil purposes) but the flatbread was both crunchy and savory. It had a sweet jam base, topped with crumbly blue cheese and finally a layer of wild mushrooms. The earth tipped on its axis and up was down. I was eating mushrooms and not perishing.

The California Grill is known for its sushi, so I opted for a course of California rolls. The extent of my California roll knowledge goes as far as getting a shrink-wrapped tray of them at the grocery store. So when I laid my eyes on the plate—which contained eight rolls, each nearly the size of a Ring Ding (you can see my culinary touchstones are only of the highest order)—I was quite surprised. The selection—tuna, crab, shrimp tempura, mango, and cucumber—was spicy, flavorful, fresh, and delicious.

The view from the restaurant is unmatched, looking out impressively over the Magic Kingdom, the Seven Seas Lagoon and the surrounding area. It's an ideal spot to catch the nighttime fireworks show, "Wishes."

TIP   *When the nightly fireworks extravaganza kicks off, the lights in the restaurant are lowered and the accompanying music is piped-in over the sound system. Guests who are not eating at the restaurant can watch the fireworks from an outdoor observation deck adjoining the restaurant.*

The main course consisted of beef in a tamarind barbecue sauce, potatoes, and a curious vegetable called "broccolini."

(It's a cross between broccoli and Chinese kale. Again, our waiter was kicking the comestible knowledge in a most impressive manner.)

The extensive dessert menu was equally as satisfying— goat cheese cheesecake with strawberry soup, sliced apples in a pastry crust, and a signature volcano cake.

If anyone tells you a meal like this is obnoxiously extravagant, just point out the fact that you'll be walking it all off while traipsing through Disney's vast property. Or simply laugh and tell them they're right.

The dining options are varied and plentiful, but may be inaccessible without proper planning. Call to make Advanced Dining Reservations as early as possible. Popular restaurants fill up quickly, even in off-peak seasons. Dining reservations can be made 180 days in advance of your arrival date. It's smart to do just that.

The obvious question is this: Who the heck knows what they're going to want to eat for dinner six months from now? It's one of the downsides of vacationing at such a popular vacation destination. The only way to gain an edge on everyone else trying to score your reservation is to do it early.

The way we approach it is to map out your week by theme park destination. Then choose a restaurant either in that park, or convenient to it. Once that's done, it's time to get on the phone with Disney Dining.

(To make advanced dining reservations, call 1-407-WDW-DINE / 1-407-939-3463.)

6 The Way of the Mousejunkie

WE HAD BEEN STANDING in the searing heat to ride The Many Adventures of Winnie the Pooh for about twenty minutes.

Fantasyland was mired in stifling humidity so thick you could almost swim in it, and the queue had ceased moving forward. It was then she started the meltdown.

"No!" she growled. "No more."

She stomped her foot. Her voiced raised a few decibels.

"This is stupid. Get me out of here right now!"

I took her hand, led her away from the line, sat her down, spoke to her in soothing tones and got her an ice cream. This seemed to defuse the situation and soon everyone was smiling. It was not unlike similar scenes replayed all across the Magic Kingdom at any given hour. Families get tired, they get hot and they get cranky. The parents snap at one another and kids lose it.

Only this was Amy. She was thirty-five at the time.

Sometimes even the most experienced Mousejunkie hits the wall. And it's then that having a fall-back plan becomes an invaluable asset.

In an effort to avoid standing in line at Walt Disney World, some travel guides will tell you to exit one attraction, turn thirty-seven degrees to the left and immediately hot-foot it to the next one on the list within seventy-two seconds. Timing and keeping to the prescribed schedule is important in this approach.

And ye shall know them by their harried look and speedy gait. You will notice that their nose will be buried in a guidebook or notepad as they jog to the next location without once looking around and taking in the minute details that make Walt Disney World the unique place that it is.

While these approaches do cut down on line time, it is not the most relaxing way to spend a vacation and it is not the proper way to get a Disney fix.

Touring the parks like a Mousejunkie does not include turning your vacation into a routine with no flexibility. Doing Disney like a Mousejunkie also doesn't include standing in queues for hours at a time. Lines are for suckers and running to keep to the plan—especially in the Florida heat and especially if you're me—is not going to happen. (Unless the destination is a buffet, in which case I've been known to move at surprising speed and with alarming focus.)

No matter where you plan to start your vacation, what you want to accomplish or what you *think* you can accomplish, let this advice guide you: You can't do it all in one trip, so don't try. It'll just leave you frustrated and tired.

It's no secret that Walt Disney World is massive. It covers roughly forty square miles, and while Disney jealously guards its attendance numbers, unofficial tallies report that more than 17 million people visited the Magic Kingdom in 2007 alone.

Walt Disney World is prepared to host many, many visitors. And at times it may seem as if every single one of them is in line in front of you at Space Mountain. That may not be the case, but I can attest that most of them pick up strollers at the Magic Kingdom main gate and then stack them in such a way that moving through Fantasyland can be nigh impossible at times.

Regardless of the ambulatory obstacles, it is possible to wade through the oft-times impenetrable tide of sticky tourists with poise and purpose.

Doing Disney like a Mousejunkie is more of a philosophy: Identify what you really want to do, figure out a plan to make sure that you do it, and anything else is gravy. Of course, I like gravy. There are secrets to maximizing the gravy. Those tips just won't include rushing unnecessarily, ramming strollers through crowds, getting pushy with other guests, or berating cast members.

If you can accept this, you can begin your journey on the path of the Mousejunkie.

Here's a look at the philosophy with which the Mousejunkies approach each park:

The Magic Kingdom

This is the original. It exudes the magic in its purest and most uncut form. It can seduce with tiny details that sneak up and whisper in your ear, and it can shake you to your core with explosive and moving examples of the fantastic.

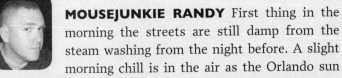

MOUSEJUNKIE RANDY First thing in the morning the streets are still damp from the steam washing from the night before. A slight morning chill is in the air as the Orlando sun has only been up for about an hour and is still climbing into the sky. Cast members from the Main Street stores beckon early morning guests with waves of their Mickey glove-clad hands. It seems as if it's too perfect and can't be real, but it is. And for me, a fellow Mousejunkie, there isn't a better way to start any day.

No matter how many times you visit the Magic Kingdom, it reveals new surprises tucked into cleverly hidden corners you may not have noticed previously. It is the shining, unblemished soul of Walt Disney World, and the most direct path to Walt and Roy's vision.

Every Walt Disney World vacation has to start at the Magic Kingdom.

There are essentially two ways to approach this park:

1. At a leisurely pace, enjoying the details
2. Go! Go! Go! Go! Eat! Go! Go! Blister! Argue! Collapse.

If it's your first trip, you'll probably be interested in hitting as many attractions as possible, which means the pace will be a little more hectic, and you'll need to get an early start. Begin your day by arriving before the park opens. Watch the opening show and then make your way inside. Don't feel like you have to run straight to the first destination. Stand at the end of Main Street USA and take it all in—get a good, long look at Cinderella Castle and everything going on around you.

The Magic Kingdom is made up of several uniquely-themed areas: Main Street USA, Fantasyland, Tomorrowland, Frontierland, Adventureland, Liberty Square, and Mickey's Toontown Fair. Unofficial sections include Get Me Out of This Insane Heat Before I Pass Outland, If That Kid Kicks Me Again I'm Going to Screamland, and I'm Not Waiting In One More Lineland.

The Mousejunkies can help with each of these themed lands.

Main Street, which was inspired by the town of Marceline, Missouri, where Walt spent part of his boyhood, will be buzzing with activity at almost any time of the day. As you enter the park and walk by the Town Hall onto Main Street, note the details: Many of the second floor windows along Main Street have names painted on them, which serve as credits for a number of the Imagineers, animators, and pioneers who contributed their skills and abilities to the Walt Disney Company. The names appear as part of fictional businesses and quite often refer to a hobby or interest the person enjoyed.

Walt Disney's window—the only one facing Cinderella Castle—is located above the ice cream parlor at the end of Main Street.

Construction throughout the park utilizes forced perspective to create the illusion of height and size, and it's put to good use in particular on Main Street. The ground-level buildings are normal sized, but the second- and third-story

MOUSEJUNKIE J The Main Street Bakery is a great place to grab a quick breakfast in the morning. It has muffins and croissants, milk and juice. You can eat relatively inexpensively there, and enjoy your breakfast in the middle of the Main Street atmosphere.

levels are progressively smaller. The effect helps complete the illusion of an idealized American thoroughfare from the early part of the 1900s.

The Magic Kingdom was constructed as a two-story structure. When you're standing on Main Street USA, you're actually on the second floor of the park. Tunnels, called "Utilidoors," run below, allowing cast members to move about without breaking the illusion on-stage, above.

TIP *For a look at the Utilidoors in action, take the Keys to the Kingdom tour. ($60 per person)*

A nice touch just to the left of Town Square between the firehouse and the Emporium is the Harmony Barber Shop. Guests can get a trim with a little flair, and quite often youngsters visiting the park get their first haircut there.

Once you're properly fed and ready to hit the attractions, head straight through the castle and into **Fantasyland**, which is packed with attractions geared for the younger set. Several of them are classics and you'll want to experience them. However, I wouldn't wait in line for any of them if it isn't necessary. And it isn't.

★ **TIP**   *Get Fantasyland out of the way early. It gets extremely congested as the day wears on, and lines can become quite long.*

Specifically, make your way to the Dumbo the Flying Elephant attraction. It loads slowly, so get it done early. The lines for Peter Pan's Flight get laughably long fairly quickly.  While it sounds like I'm advocating running from attraction-to-attraction at this point, you have to weigh the wait time against the fact that most of these are very short experiences. Standby wait times can quickly reach sixty minutes or longer, and in the case of Peter Pan's Flight, the ride itself is just shy of three minutes. If you get delayed, use Fastpass on this attraction.

Here's a list of attractions where Fastpass is available in the Magic Kingdom:

➤ Big Thunder Mountain Railroad
➤ Jungle Cruise
➤ Peter Pan's Flight
➤ Splash Mountain
➤ Buzz Lightyear's Space Ranger Spin
➤ Mickey's PhilharMagic
➤ Space Mountain
➤ The Many Adventures of Winnie the Pooh
➤ Stitch's Great Escape!

A quick tour through Fantasyland will include It's a Small World, Snow White's Scary Adventure, The Many

Adventures of Winnie the Pooh, Mad Teacups, and Mickey's Philharmagic.

> **TIP** *No two horses on Cinderella's Royal Carousel, located in Fantasyland, are the same. The most coveted, Cinderella's horse, is designated by a golden ribbon tied around its tail.*

Tomorrowland was given a makeover in 1994 when Imagineers opted to avoid trying to keep up with constantly-evolving images of the future. A retro look and feel replaced the dated-looking district, which is home to one of the most popular attractions in the Magic Kingdom, Space Mountain. As with any of the massively popular attractions, Fastpass is recommended.

A loop through Tomorrowland will bring you through Buzz Lightyear's Space Ranger Spin, the Astro Orbiter, Stitch's Great Escape, the Tomorrowland Indy Speedway, Walt Disney's Carousel of Progress (voiced by writer/actor Jean Shepherd) and the Monsters Inc. Laugh Floor. Guests can text-message a joke for use in this show as they wait in line.

> **TIP** *To boost your score on Buzz Lightyear's Space Ranger Spin, located in Tomorrowland, shoot for smaller, far away targets and anything that moves. Specifically, aim for the back of the robot's left wrist in the first room for a 100,000-point bonus. Target Zurg when you arrive at Planet Z and hit the bottom of his space scooter for another 100,000 points.*

If your party is in a hurry or you're running out of time, consider dropping Stitch's Great Escape from your touring plans. It is consistently panned by guests and ranks lower than most other attractions in its general vicinity. It's a retrofit of the Extra-TERRORestrial Alien Encounter attraction, and retains much of what made that too frightening for children: It's dark, loud, and you're strapped into a seat and can't move.

While it may not look like much, the Tomorrowland Transit Authority (TTA) offers a relaxing, breezy tour and a chance to get off your feet for ten minutes. There's rarely a line (if there is one, it moves quickly) and you can get a look at the wait times at other Tomorrowland attractions from your lofty perch.

A quick cut back across the Castle Hub will bring you to **Adventureland**, where such classics as the Enchanted Tiki Room, the Jungle Cruise, the Swiss Family Tree House, and Pirates of the Caribbean reside. The Magic Carpets of Aladdin are here, as well, and are an almost identical attraction to Dumbo the Flying Elephant, in that the ride vehicles go up in the air and circle for approximately ninety seconds.

Next door in **Frontierland** are a few of the park's major attractions: Big Thunder Mountain Railroad and Splash Mountain. The generally accepted approach here is to get a Fastpass for one, and get in the standby line for the other.

The Country Bear Jamboree and Tom Sawyer Island will lead you back toward Liberty Square, for the Hall of Presidents, the Liberty Square Riverboat, and the Haunted Mansion.

TIP *If you arrive at the park during the daily 3 P.M. parade, hop on the train at Main Street Station and take it to Frontierland. You'll miss the crowds and be half-way across the park in minutes.*

Keep in mind: If there is a line longer than a few minutes, keep walking. There's always something a few steps farther with a shorter wait. You can always return when crowds are lighter (like during the 3 P.M. parade or during the nightly Wishes fireworks display).

Mickey's Toontown Fair gives youngsters a great opportunity to interact with their favorite characters up-close and personal. The lines to meet Mickey and Minnie are longest in the morning. Try visiting the Judge's Tent to meet the big cheese later in the day.

Kids can also ride the Barnstormer at Goofy's Wiseacre Farm (a kiddie-sized roller coaster) and play in Mickey's Country House, Minnie's Country House, and Donald's Boat here. There's a train station located at the back of Mickey's Toontown Fair, which is a quick and convenient option for getting back to the front of the park.

A daily 3 P.M. parade steps off (currently the Celebrate a Dream Come True parade) and on select nights guests can catch the Spectromagic parade and the Wishes fireworks extravaganza.

The Walt Disney World Railroad is an alternative way to get from one side of the park to the other. There are train stations at the main gate at Main Street and at the opposite end of the park in ToonTown. It's also a quick way to get to

MOUSEJUNKIE WALT I like to watch Spectromagic and the Share a Dream Come True parade and Wishes from right next to the Partners Statue. It's located in the center of the hub directly in front of Cinderella Castle. And when these things kick off I want to be right in front of everything. You're far enough back where you can appreciate what they're doing, and yet it's framed by the Castle.

Frontierland. If your priority is to get to Splash Mountain or Big Thunder Mountain Railroad quickly, it can be a speedy way to traverse the park.

TIP *If you or someone you are traveling with is celebrating a birthday, stop at City Hall and get a birthday pin from guest relations. You'll be greeted by dozens of guests and cast members by name throughout the day, and sometimes it will result in some extra magic.*

On my fortieth birthday, Amy and I rented a Boston Whaler motorboat from the Polynesian Resort. We putted around the Seven Seas Lagoon for an hour. (The Whaler has a modest engine, which precludes me from saying that we "roared around the Seven Seas Lagoon for an hour.") When we returned to the resort to pay for the rental, the cast member noticed my birthday pin.

"Is it really your birthday?" he asked.

I said it was.

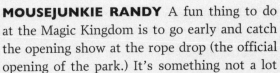

MOUSEJUNKIE RANDY A fun thing to do at the Magic Kingdom is to go early and catch the opening show at the rope drop (the official opening of the park.) It's something not a lot of people see, it's not on any map, and it's free. It really brings you the whole atmosphere of the park in one show. That in itself makes it worth getting up early.

Once you're inside, take your time on Main Street. The cast members are outside welcoming everyone because at that time of day no one is shopping. Everyone is heading straight for the Castle. Just stop for a second and look around and listen. Everything has a theme and is put together very well. You don't have to be on a ride to enjoy what the Imagineers have done to make it a complete experience.

"And finally, don't wait in line. Try the attraction you walk by that has no line. Everyone sees there's no crowd and assumes the attraction must stink. Trust me, every attraction has something to offer.

"Then happy birthday," he said. "The rental is on me."

This was the first of several surprises during that birthday trip, which included free desserts, free drinks, and a completely unexpected front-of-the-line escort at the Great Movie Ride at Disney's Hollywood Studios.

Approach the Magic Kingdom slowly. It allows for a more relaxed pace, and the opportunity to notice the details Imagineers created through the years.

TIP   *If it's particularly hot, visit Mickey's Philharmagic, the Hall of Presidents or the Carousel of Progress for a break. These are among the longer shows that offer a place to sit down in a dark, air-conditioned theater.*

Epcot

Originally based on Walt Disney's plan for a perfect community, Epcot has grown beyond what he could have possibly imagined.

Every day at Epcot brings with it a renewed vision of a world of cooperative harmony. The park throws open its arms each morning, offering guests a look at new technologies, providing them with innovative ideas and exciting them with a glimpse into other cultures. Every night it sends visitors home inspired by Epcot's message of exploration, innovation, and hope.

And in my case it might also send you home with a belly full of margaritas. But that doesn't lessen the impact of its core values.

Epcot is separated into two major sections: **Future World** and the **World Showcase**. It's fairly large and can handle crowds much better than the other parks. But there's only one way to start the day here: Head straight to Soarin', located in the Land pavilion, get a Fastpass and then get right in the standby line. This allows you to ride the attraction, exit, and then ride it again at the Fastpass return time if you are so inclined.

MOUSEJUNKIE WALT Soarin' is one of my all-time favorite rides for a very specific reason—it fulfills Walt Disney's original goal. It's a ride I, my grandfather, and my four-year-old nephew all went on together. It's something families can do together, and it's amazing in that respect.

TIP *If you're not going to use your Fastpass for Soarin', offer it to guests coming into the attraction. Once you leave the Land pavilion, there's not much motivation to return, and you won't need it. Besides, it's just a nice thing to do.*

Head back across the park to Test Track (choose the single rider line if you don't mind riding with someone other than your party) and then Mission: Space.

It's no secret that I'm a chicken when it comes to the more thrilling attractions. The first time I had an opportunity to experience Mission: Space was when I was offered a personal tour of it by a Disney public relations cast member. I was to meet him in front of the attraction and then we'd head inside.

I arrived early and struck up a conversation with a cast member stationed at the entrance. I asked him just how scary this virtual trip to the outer galaxy actually was. He assured me it was easily the most intense attraction on Disney property.

"The Rock 'n' Roller Coaster can put some pretty good G-forces on you," he said. "But only Mission: Space can put them there and *maintain* them."

I was having second thoughts about even showing up when my PR contact arrived.

"I'm not too sure I want to ride this," I told him.

He was polite and maintained a completely professional attitude. But I sensed a look in his eyes that said, "You big chicken—what the heck am I doing here?"

I read the look on his face and opted to suck it up and act like a big boy.

"On second thought, let's go on in," I said.

With that, I was given a tour of the queue area, front-of-the-line treatment, and a few tips from my contact, who had experienced it more than a dozen times. Specifically: Keep looking straight forward and pay attention to the narrator. Actually completing the tasks asked of you in the rocket keeps your mind off the fact that you're being flung in a circle on the end of a centrifuge.

I'm glad I gave it a shot. It's an exhilarating ride that'll get your pulse racing without actually achieving escape velocity. Plus the PR contact bought dinner at the California Grill that night.

Mission: Space now offers guests two ride options: the original, and a more mild experience that cuts out the centrifuge element. Upon entering the queue, a cast member will ask which side you'd prefer. He or she will hand you a red card or a green card. Red indicates you prefer the original, more intense ride, while a green card indicates that you enjoy crocheting potholders and watching reruns of the *Golden Girls* for excitement.

I found the milder side to be only slightly less disorienting, since the 3-D effects are what made me feel queasy.

Mission: Space is one of four major attractions in the park. Once you've got Soarin', Test Track, and Mission: Space out of the way, there's only Spaceship Earth between you and a pint of ale at the United Kingdom pavilion in the World Showcase.

TIP *If Fastpasses are unavailable or inconvenient, consider using the single rider line at Test Track and Mission: Space. While you may not sit with your touring party, it will dramatically decrease your wait time.*

Here's a list of attractions that offer Fastpass at Epcot:

➤ Soarin'
➤ Test Track
➤ Mission: Space
➤ Maelstrom (Norway)
➤ Living With the Land
➤ Honey, I Shrunk the Audience

Spaceship Earth, Epcot's iconic golf ball-shaped sphere, has always been one of my favorite attractions. It's dark, cool, slow-moving and it tells an interesting tale. It also retains the innate charm in attractions that feature audio animatronics.

My most frequent travel partner, Amy, loathes it.

"I expect a lot better from something that represents an entire theme park," she said. "It's old, dusty, and it stops a lot."

Recently, Spaceship Earth underwent a fairly extensive rehab that inserted a few new scenes, an interactive element, and gave it a much-needed interior cleaning. As a result the lines are now much longer than they once were. Consider inserting this into your touring plan as you walk from Soarin' to Test Track.

TIP *On particularly hot days, be sure to visit Ellen's Energy Adventure. It's air conditioned, dark, and lasts about forty minutes. Several of the Mousejunkies have been known to take advantage of these factors to steal a quick nap. Though not all at the same time.*

Wander around Future World, visit the newly-rehabbed Living Seas, shop and enjoy the Fountain of Nations until the World Showcase opens or until you get hungry.

Besides, Test Track is a good ride first thing in the morning. It's cool out, and it wakes everybody up. And once you've got the E-ticket rides out of the way, you won't have to wait for much else in the park. It's just shows and the World Showcase.

TIP *Take advantage of Disney's PhotoPass. Digital pictures taken by Disney's photographers are linked to a free card containing a barcode and serial number. Guests log-on to the PhotoPass web site using the serial number and can*

> **MOUSEJUNKIE RANDY** Right now, anyone going to Epcot is running to Soarin' first. And that's still the best way to do it. It's really the only ride at Epcot where you *have* to get a Fastpass. There's either going to be a two-hour wait, or they'll run out of Fastpasses.

view or purchase the pictures for up to thirty days. The great aspect of PhotoPass is that every member of the touring party is included in the photo—no one is left holding the camera. On the downside, the photos are exorbitantly expensive. PhotoPass is available in all four theme parks.

The World Showcase boasts eleven pavilions representing various countries from around the world. Clockwise, in order, they are: Mexico, Norway, China, Germany, Italy, the American Adventure, Japan, Morocco, France, the United Kingdom, and Canada. Each country's pavilion is staffed by cast members who are from that particular country. It's a great way to get a taste of different cultures—both figuratively and literally.

If you're traveling with children, take advantage of the World Showcase Kidcot Fun Stops. Kids are presented with a mask which they can color on and decorate at craft areas normally located deep within each of the pavilions. This forces guests to really visit each pavilion, talk to cast members from that country, and it gives kids something to do in

MOUSEJUNKIE RANDY You don't really need a plan to tour the World Showcase. Some people will tell you it's better to go counter-clockwise to avoid crowds—but that's really not the case. Just go in and explore every country. Check out the little corners. That's where you'll find the most rewarding details.

an environment that otherwise has little in the way of traditional theme park rides.

And make sure to catch the street performers throughout the day. They're some of the best free shows in all of Disney World. They're not on any map, but they're all fun and interesting.

The World Tour:

Mexico: Margaritas and an air-conditioned shopping area make this a great place to escape the midday sun. The pavilion's ride, El Rio del Tiempo, was once a welcome break from the walking, but its updated version, Gran Fiesta Tour Starring the Three Caballeros, is a rather loathsome retrofit. Kids might find the Donald Duck storyline engaging, but it has stripped the attraction of any dignity and seems to run opposite of the park's theme. It teaches guests nothing about Mexico.

Norway: Maelstrom is a dark ride, of sorts, where guests are taken on a Viking boat into a tour of Norway's past and present. A collection of audio animatronic Nordic warriors, polar bears, and trolls drop in along the way. The journey ends in a re-creation of a small Norwegian fishing village. Guests are ushered through a theater where a short film about the country is shown. In addition, Norway has the most statuesque and usually blondest cast members.

A friend of the family is from Norway, and taught me the only Norwegian phrase I believe I will ever need: *"Jaeg snakker, ikke Norsk."* (I do not know how to speak Norwegian.)

I try it out on whatever cast member is working at the gift cart near the bakery on every single trip. It's usually met with an uncomfortable smile, but on one occasion the cast member taught me a few other phrases. Amy, on the other hand, knows I'm itching to say it, and has grown weary of this tradition.

TIP *Impress your friends—point out the "hidden Mickey" in the mural facing the loading area in Maelstrom. He's sitting in the Viking ship with the striped sails.*

China: The children's acrobat show is impressive and should not be missed. There's a 360-degree-style movie, *Reflections of China*, and the current manager of the gift shop in China is extremely friendly, talkative, and a pretty good salesman. He convinced us to buy a parasol when he wrote my daughter's name on it in Chinese.

A Chinese parasol was the last thing I needed. But the interaction with the manager was more than worth it.

TIP *The temple in China is acoustically perfect. Stand in the direct center and listen to yourself speak. You'll hear your own voice as others hear you.*

Germany: Take part in the ongoing Oktoberfest spirit by grabbing a brew and watching for the glockenspiel that overlooks St. Georges Platz. A miniature train and village makes for a great place to take a brief rest.

Italy: The architecture in the Italy pavilion is remarkable, and the World Showcase Players provide great entertainment. The landscaping here includes olive trees and grapevines, adding a very evocative feel to the reproduction of St. Mark's Square. Where Alfredo's once offered solid Italian fare, there's a new, even more expensive restaurant—even by Disney standards—called Tutto Italia in its place.

The American Adventure: A multimedia presentation, the American Adventure takes guests on a trip through America's history. It is narrated by audio animatronic figures of Benjamin Franklin and Mark Twain. It's presented in an auditorium where sets and characters rise up from beneath the stage to portray scenes from different historical periods. The theme, "Golden Dream," is moving and this show is not to be missed.

Maybe just as importantly, this is the area where guests can get a funnel cake.

TIP *Do not miss the Voices of Liberty, an a cappella group, which perform in the rotunda of the American Adventure, an acoustically superior venue. If you visit around Christmas, the Voices of Liberty will perform classic Christmas carols. Check your park map for times.*

Japan: Perhaps the one country that engages me the least, Japan offers shopping and dining. That said, the Matsuriza, or traditional Taiko drummers, are part of the natural Epcot soundtrack. The sounds of the drums echo all the way across the lagoon, mixing with the piercing horns of the Friendships that ferry guests around the World Showcase and to and from the Boardwalk Resort area to create a background hum found only at Epcot.

Architecturally, however, it is among the more stunning pavilions in the World Showcase. The castle in Japan is a replica of the Shirasagi-Jo, a seventeenth-century fortress considered one of the most well-preserved of its like.

Morocco: The winding alleyways that draw visitors deeper into the Morocco pavilion are so well done, guests will almost swear they've been transported there. The Treasures of Morocco is a tour designed to teach guests more about the culture, people and history of this north African land. This type of tour is unique to the Morocco pavilion.

Plus—belly dancers!

France: I was once one of those guests who actually asked directions to get to the Eiffel Tower. (Hint: You can't. It's a prop located on the roof near the back of the pavilion. It's visible from all over the park, serving as a great visual, but nothing more.) People-watching from inside Chefs de France is among the best in all of Epcot, and the film, *Impressions de France*, is both moving and informative.

The fountain outside Chefs de France is lit up at night, creating one of the most atmospheric spots in the park. My five-year-old daughter asked for a penny as we stood next to the fountain. She approached the bubbling waters and said, in complete innocence and earnestness, "I hope Mama and Daddy never have to work again so we can come to Disney World every day"—and tossed the penny in.

★ **TIP**   *The replica Eiffel Tower stands 103 feet tall.*

The United Kingdom: Pints of ale in the Rose and Crown Pub can signify the second to last stop when "drinking around the world," but it also provides a relaxing stop along the World Showcase loop. A picturesque garden tucked in the back of the pavilion is another fantastic spot for a breather. But don't get the impression the UK pavilion is all about relaxation. British Invasion, a Beatles-inspired act, provides toe-tapping renditions of tunes made famous by the Fab Four. They perform several times daily in a gazebo just off a large garden area.

★ **TIP**   *Photo opportunities with Winnie the Pooh characters are often available in the back of the Toy Soldier shop. It's an out-of-the-way location with very little foot traffic, so the lines are often quite short.*

Canada: A waterfall splashing down a canyon, ornate gardens, and totem polls serve to teach visitors that Canada is much more than hockey rinks and lumberjacks. The Circle-Vision 360 movie, *O Canada!*, hosted by Martin Short was

MOUSEJUNKIE WALT Other countries should learn from Canada. The movie update they did is great. It teaches you about the country of Canada and you get to learn about the people who live there. Some of the other movies are sorely lacking in this respect. They feel old and tired. Whereas Canada—they did it right.

updated in 2007 and goes even further to show the many faces of our neighbor to the north.

Originally shot in 1979, the old *O Canada!* had grown tired, and the song was maddeningly repetitive. I always expected more from the country that gave us Rush. The updated version revisits the theme, which is now sung by Canadian Idol Eva Avila.

TIP *The path around the World Showcase is 1.2 miles long. Consider taking a Friendship from one side to the other if you're beginning to grow tired. It's a relaxing way to traverse the World Showcase.*

For those drinking around the world: You have reached the finish line (assuming you went clockwise.) Please gather your things and move quietly to the exit. While it does seem like a fun way to travel the World Showcase, I've seen the results. And it's not pretty.

Drinking around the world (much like eating around the world) involves ordering a drink at each of the countries and moving on. Participants must complete the circuit before the park closes. In Mexico, it's an exciting start to the day. By Italy it's riotously funny. By the United Kingdom it's just sloppy.

Each country in the World Showcase has a table service restaurant and a counter service option. For example, Le Cellier, in Canada, is one of the more popular table service restaurants. It can be difficult to get an Advanced Dining Reservation (ADR), but if you can swing it, do so. On the other hand, while it is good, it's not worth rearranging an entire day around. Just don't expect to get in if you walk up without making an ADR.

The fish and chips at the Rose and Crown Pub are a deep-fried treat that goes well with a pint, while the Biergarten in Germany is a chance to enjoy some oompa music in a communal setting.

On the opposite end of the spectrum, I advise people to avoid the San Angel Inn in the Mexico pavilion. It's reportedly a corporate cousin to a Mexico City restaurant of the same name, which dates back to 1692. That may be the case, but I also suspect that's the last time anyone took a close look at what they were serving.

The atmosphere is fantastic, with the feel of a nighttime outdoor patio in the shadow of a Mexican pyramid. The service is adequate. The food, on the other hand, is where this particular restaurant falls short. During our last meal there (which will be our last meal there) the beef was bone dry, the tortillas tasted stale, the chips were slow to refill, and the presentation looked as if a hose filled with a mixture of mud and beans was being fired at the plates from across the kitchen.

By all means, however, enjoy the wonderful offerings in the pavilion. Ride the Gran Fiesta Tour Starring the Three Caballeros (a spit-shine/refitting of El Rio del Tiempo), be sure to catch a performance by Mariachi Cobre, and visit the Kidcot stop. If you start feeling the urge for some food, simply exit the main building and cross the road to the Cantina San Angel.

It's there that we discovered what I consider to be the best counter service option in Epcot. Sure, it isn't much more than tacos, burritos and nacho fare, but pair it with a margarita and you've got a successful combination. Add to it the best outdoor dining spot at Epcot, and it has become a necessary stop during our visits.

Six of the Mousejunkies, all arriving separately from destinations ranging from New England to Las Vegas, met up at Cantina San Angel late one afternoon during a coordinated trip in May. Amy and I arrived early, staked out a table right on the water and awaited our companions' arrival. Within an hour, margaritas were flowing freely, cheesy nachos were had all around and as the sun slowly set over Walt Disney World, we settled in for the finest nighttime display in all of the resort, IllumiNations: Reflections of Earth.

As the natural light grew dim, the stars over the Florida sky began to blink on, and massive torches that line the lagoon blazed to life. We were afforded a front-row seat to my single favorite attraction, show, or display in all of Walt Disney World.

IllumiNations: Reflections of Earth is a fireworks/laser/pyrotechnic show set to music and performed every night

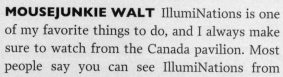 **MOUSEJUNKIE WALT** IllumiNations is one of my favorite things to do, and I always make sure to watch from the Canada pavilion. Most people say you can see IllumiNations from anywhere, and that is true. But to get the best view, head for Canada—and here's why: First, there are not a lot of trees in the way. More importantly, you're looking across the lagoon at more countries than anywhere else in the park. Why does this matter? During a certain point in the display the countries are lit up by brilliant white lights. So when the white lights come on, you get a much better view. I've watched IllumiNations from all over the park, and when you're on the other side near Japan or Germany, you look across and see Canada and England. That's it. It's not as good. If you're in Canada you can see the American pavilion and everything to the left of it from there.

over the World Showcase Lagoon. It's viewable from anywhere in the World Showcase, though a few locations are more sought-after than others.

Just before the show is launched, the lights around the park go down, leaving only the lagoon torches burning. A narrator sets the scene:

Good evening. On behalf of Walt Disney World, the place where dreams come true, we welcome all of you to Epcot and World Showcase. We've gathered here tonight, around the fire, as people of all lands have gathered for thousands and thousands of years before us; to share the light and to share a story—an amazing story, as old as time itself but still being written. And though each of us has our own individual stories to tell, a true adventure emerges when we bring them all together as one. We hope you enjoy our story tonight; Reflections of Earth.

Low drums begin to sound as a single rocket hurtles through the night sky. When it explodes it sets off a display of fire, sound, fury, and hope in three acts: Chaos, order, and celebration. The music, reflecting each act, is alternately wild, introspective, and triumphant.

Between being tossed around by attractions such as Test Track and Mission: Space, walking endlessly through the World Showcase and ultimately being serenaded by an inspiring performance of hope, I have never left Epcot feeling anything less than completely exhausted and happy.

Disney's Animal Kingdom

I'm about as likely to go to Africa as I am to run the Boston Marathon in cha-cha shoes. That is to say that while it's not entirely impossible, it's highly unlikely.

And yet every time I walk through the entrance of Disney's Animal Kingdom, I'm convinced that's exactly what I've done. Guests are slowly transported from central Florida into equatorial Africa. Heading slowly uphill through a jungle like setting, visitors emerge from a cavernous structure to clear the top of the hill and are rewarded with a jaw-dropping view of the Tree of Life.

A massive, fourteen-story creation, the tree was engineered from an oil platform and has been the park's icon since opening in 1998. Disney set its Imaginers loose on it, and the result is a rather awe-inspiring piece of art that features more than 325 animals carved into its Kynar surface.

> ⭐ **TIP** *Ten artists worked full-time for eighteen months to carve the 325 animals into the Tree of Life, which is topped by more than 103,000 artificial leaves.*

The Tree of Life houses the 3D film, *It's Tough to Be a Bug*. It's a fun romp featuring characters from the Disney/Pixar film, *A Bug's Life*. But be warned: I have yet to catch a showing of this film where at least three children do not freak out in a fit of screaming terror. It's not a frightening film, by any means, but there are a few unexpected tactile surprises, an army of marauding spiders and pitch-black moments that seem to unsettle the young ones.

They key to this park is pacing. Go slowly. There are details around every corner. The buildings in Harambe—the park's African village—are suitably aged. The paths are scarred by cracks and animal tracks. The signs in Anandupur—the Indian village—are dry and faded. And wherever you find a patch of green, you're likely to find a new animal to observe and learn about.

> ⭐ **TIP** *Consider splitting your Animal Kingdom tour into a "scream" day and a "see" day. This will allow you to attack the bigger attractions one day (Expedition: Everest, Dinosaur, Kilimanjaro Safari, Kali River Rapids), and then spend a day walking around and enjoying the quieter aspects of the park,*

like Conservation Station, the Maharajah Jungle Trek,
Pangani Forest Exploration Trail, and Flights of Wonder.

The best approach for Disney's Animal Kingdom is to forget it's a theme park, for the most part. It's not about rushing from one thing to the next (with a couple of minor exceptions). It's about taking it all in.

Besides, if you insist on hoofing it from one attraction to the next at top speed, you risk incurring one of the most objectionable penalties imaginable on Disney property. I refer, of course, to chafing.

This isn't your run-of-the-mill, "I just walked around the mall in July" chafing. This is an aggressive, flesh-searing strain of chafing unique to Southern states.

This particularly painful affliction is not relegated strictly to fat people or individuals with questionable fashion sense. It can strike anyone in the Florida heat, and when it strikes, it can be debilitating. The pain involved with such chafing is unique and mentally scarring. During a vacation built around walking, it can cripple even the best-laid plans.

There is only one way to combat the chafing, and its closely-related cousin, the blisters, and that is with a liberal application of Bodyglide.

Bodyglide is your friend. It completely prevents chafing and blisters. It comes in a stick resembling deodorant and is applied in much the same manner. Order it before you go on your trip, do not forget to pack it, and slather it on liberally each morning before attacking the day. It can, literally, save a vacation.

Feel free to carry it with you in case further applications are needed, but quite often I've found that an early morning coating is enough to keep the thigh fires at bay.

While the key to touring Animal Kingdom successfully is to take it at a leisurely pace, there is a pair of attractions specifically worth visiting, and they get busy early. The two gate-busting attractions are located at opposite ends of the park: Expedition Everest—a roller coaster housed in a massive recreation of the world's highest mountain, and Kilimanjaro Safari—a guided tour through an African savannah.

The best approach is to pick one, go directly to it and get a Fastpass, and then walk across the park to the other.

Of course, this means a great deal of speedy walking first thing in the morning. And since I'm a huge chicken when it comes to thrilling rides, I just head straight for Kilimanjaro Safari. When I'm with people who are interested in tempting the Yeti, we split up. One of our group gets Fastpasses for one attraction, while the rest get in the queue for the other. We all meet up and everyone gets to do both fairly early in the day. Fastpasses are available for both of these attractions and Expedition Everest has a single rider line—which will cut your wait time down dramatically.

Here is a list of attractions that offer Fastpass at Disney's Animal Kingdom:

➤ Expedition Everest
➤ Kilimanjaro Safari
➤ Dinosaur

➤ It's Tough to Be a Bug!
➤ Kali River Rapids
➤ Primeval Whirl

MOUSEJUNKIE WALT When you go to Disney World, you have to realize it's not solely about crazy thrill rides. What makes Disney so special is how they immerse you into the theming. Expedition Everest is great, but it's walking around and seeing all the artifacts they brought back from Tibet that makes it so real. When you go on Dr. Doom's Fear Fall across town at Universal's Islands of Adventure, there's no theme at all. It's one of my favorite rides, but it goes like this: They strap you in, they shoot you up, it scares the life out of you and it's over. It's a thrill, but that's it.

TIP *Head to the Kilimanjaro Safari early in the morning, or very late in the day. If you do it in the morning, they've just let animals out of enclosures into the display areas. The animals are wide awake, and they get them out there by using food so they're active. At the end of the day the animals are in transition, being prepared to be led back into the enclosures for the night, and you'll see a lot more activity.*

Don't get too caught up in the sexy stuff. I'd be perfectly happy if I didn't get to see any of the bigger attractions as long as the Festival of the Lion King was on the schedule.

MOUSEJUNKIE RANDY The two theatrical shows, Festival of the Lion King and Finding Nemo: The Musical, are great. However, don't feel like you have to break your neck to cram both of them in to a day. If you have to choose one, make it Festival of the Lion King. It is the superior production.

A colorful, boisterous pageant combining elements of the Broadway production with the feel of a tribal celebration, Festival of the Lion King is a musical production featuring acrobats, dancers, wire ballet, puppets, audience participation, and some of the songs made famous by the film.

Disney's Hollywood Studios

Walking through the main gates of this park takes guests on a trip back to 1930s Hollywood, when starlets were glamorous and leading men talked tough.

At the dedication of the park in 1989, then-CEO Michael Eisner described it this way:

"The World you have entered was created by The Walt Disney Company and is dedicated to Hollywood—not a place on a map, but a state of mind that exists wherever people dream and wonder and imagine, a place where illusion and reality are fused by technological magic. We welcome you to a Hollywood that never was—and always will be."

The key attractions at Disney's Hollywood Studios are Twilight Zone Tower of Terror, the Rock 'n' Roller Coaster, Star Tours, and the new Toy Story Mania!

Toy Story Mania! is an interactive attraction where guests don 3-D glasses and board spinning vehicles to try their hand at carnival-style midway games.

The good thing about the Tower of Terror and the Rock 'n' Roller Coaster is even though they're massively popular; Fastpasses are usually available until 2 or 3 P.M.—even on a very busy day.

Here's how to make the most of your day and experience each of these main attractions:

➤ Head straight for Toy Story Mania! and ride it. It's located on Pixar Place behind the Great Movie Ride.
➤ Turn right around and head back to Sunset Boulevard and get a Fastpass for the Twilight Zone Tower of Terror. Walk right next door and ride the Rock 'n' Roller Coaster and then return to the Tower of Terror for your Fastpass return time. A quick jaunt across to Star Tours and the big four are taken care of.

Here's a list of attractions that offer Fastpass at Disney's Hollywood Studios:

➤ Toy Story Mania!
➤ The Twilight Zone Tower of Terror
➤ Rock 'n' Roller Coaster
➤ The Voyage of the Little Mermaid
➤ Star Tours

An alternate touring plan would put the park's thrill rides first. Here's where you have to make a decision—do you want to be a thrill-seeker or a gamer? If you want to get your adrenaline going, hit the Tower of Terror and the Rock 'n' Roller Coaster first. If you want to try your hand at virtual carnival games, head straight for Pixar Place.

After that, your day gets a lot more relaxing. The only other real line that develops is at the Great Movie Ride. It was once the marquee attraction, and people still tend to congregate there because of its central location, but it does not warrant any kind of wait.

This is not to say the rest of Disney's Hollywood Studios is line-free. This is Walt Disney World, after all, and the line at the popcorn cart can become unwieldy very quickly.

With any luck, however, you'll be able to see the rest of the park without to much trouble: The Beauty and the Beast Stage Show, the Back Lot Tour, Lights, Motors, Action! Extreme Stunt Show, the Animation Tour, the Voyage of the Little Mermaid and, if you've got any youngsters with you, Playhouse Disney can all handle large crowds easily.

If you're a Disney fanatic or are interested in Disney history, make sure to walk through Walt Disney: One Man's Dream—a museum dedicated to the life of Walt Disney. It allows guests to look through photos, models, artifacts, and recreations of key moments in Disney's life. It ends with a short film narrated by Julie Andrews.

As the day wears on, you may have to decide if you want to see action, or if you'd rather see things explode. The Indiana Jones Stunt Spectacular provides action sequences based around the characters from the first movie, while the Lights, Motors, Action! Extreme Stunt Show features fast cars, gunfire and explosions. Both handle large crowds well, so if a line has formed, just move along until the show starts seating guests. With a little planning it's not difficult to catch both stunt shows in one day.

At 3 P.M. the park's new Toy Story Block Party Bash comes to life. A stage show/parade, it moves through the streets of Disney's Hollywood Studios before setting up performances in several areas throughout the park. Cast members perform dance numbers, interactive contests, and songs before packing the show up and moving along.

TIP *It's worth trying to get a spot a little early for the Block Party Bash. Stake out an area near Sorcerer Mickey's hat (the giant, blue hat at the end of Hollywood Boulevard). Get a spot on the right-hand side. This will allow you to view the performance without looking straight into the sun. Additionally, the right-hand side offers a little more protection from the sun—which will fry you no matter what time of year it is.*

A day at Disney's Hollywood Studios always ends with the nightly performance of Fantasmic. Good (Mickey and friends) clashes with evil (assorted Disney villains) in a fireworks/laser/hydrotechnic show set to dramatic music and vivid lighting.

It's always crowded, and planning to sit in the center of the theater requires arriving at least an hour before show time. The Hollywood Hills Amphitheatre features metal benches that surround the performance area in a semi-circle.

Your early arrival may get you a good, centrally-located seat, but it's also going to guarantee you a numb rear end.

Avoid the wasted time in line by booking a Fantasmic dinner package. This allows you to dine at specific times, and then arrive just before show time in a reserved seating area.

> **TIP** *Many people will advise you to line up for Fantasmic extremely early. Here's why they're wrong: If it's ten minutes until the show starts and they're still letting people in, then by all means take a seat. The later you get there, the more likely it is that you will able to sit near the back and to the right. This is important for two reasons: You can see fine from anywhere in the amphitheatre, and—more importantly—you'll be near the exit.*

The Hollywood Hills Amphitheatre seats nearly ten thousand people. And when show is over, everyone leaves at once. The entire crowd is funneled into a single walkway, which is then split into to main exits. Being near the exit when the show ends can save a lot of time and aggravation.

Mouse Droppings

Eventually you're going to have to go to the bathroom at
 Disney World. It's a function of giant turkey legs and expensive soda vs. your bladder. At some point your bladder will surrender and you'll be looking for a room to rest in.

MOUSEJUNKIE CAROL The best bathroom in the Magic Kingdom would have to be the first one as you walk into the park near guest relations. Just walk through the front gates and bear right at the hub. It's the one guests come across first, so it's kept pretty clean and cool.

The worst bathroom in the Magic Kingdom would be the one going from Fantasyland into Frontierland, right after the Peter Pan attraction. It's very stuffy, and I believe it to be the diaper-changing mecca of Magic Kingdom.

The bathrooms located at the Lights, Motors, Action! Stunt Car Spectacular are the best in Disney's Hollywood Studios theme park. They are the newest ones on the property and really only get used when there are people going to see the show. The worst one is a tie between the bathrooms on the right as you first enter the park and the one right before the Tower of Terror attraction. Both seem a little stuffy and I find the odor to be quite unpleasant.

The bathroom on the far side of the Odyssey building is the best one in Epcot. Although a little out of the way, it is cool and reasonably clean. You'll want to avoid the restroom behind the American Pavilion restaurant. Not only is it a hike to get to, but always seems crowded and hot.

Here's a little restroom insight: On New Year's Eve there are no good bathrooms at Epcot. All of them are extremely crowded, and due to the amount of drinking that occurs at that particular park you can imagine how unpleasant it is.

MOUSEJUNKIE DEB My pick of the best bathroom in all of Walt Disney World is the one off the Boardwalk Inn/Villas lobby. It's always cool in there, you never have to wait (a rarity for women in public restrooms). It has no offensive smells, and it is always stocked with a huge basket of dry, rolled facecloths available at the sinks, and a separate basket underneath to discard.

After doing your business and leaving with a renewed sense of energy, where else would you want to walk out to than the brightly lit, always air-conditioned, nostalgically decorated, 1920s music-filled Boardwalk lobby? On a lucky day, you may get even a whiff of food coming from the dining establishments below.

Although they're a necessity, I'd have to say any pool-adjacent bathroom is among the worst. At the risk of sounding snotty, the more value the resort, the more I'd avoid it. Not that the bathrooms themselves are in bad shape, but people are walking in there barefoot. Hello—it's a public restroom. Shoes, please!

There are all manner of Disney restrooms that dot the theme parks. They range from shining examples of Disney efficiency in which to seek relief, to slimy pits of filth that leave guests questioning whether we reside in a civilized world or not.

Fear not—the Mousejunkies have fanned out across Walt Disney World to test, review and report back on the various facilities offered throughout the property.

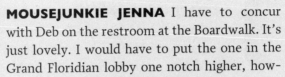

MOUSEJUNKIE JENNA I have to concur with Deb on the restroom at the Boardwalk. It's just lovely. I would have to put the one in the Grand Floridian lobby one notch higher, however. Most of the restrooms in Deluxe resorts are great, but the restrooms closest to 'Ohana and Boma seem to be the exceptions there. The one at Boma is just nothing special, and the one at 'Ohana is way too small for the area it serves and it tends to get soggy and messy fast.

I think the best in-park restrooms are the ones in the Animal Kingdom, because I'm partial to the Xcelerator hand dryers; but don't use the one near Kali River Rapids unless you want wet feet.

The worst restroom is the one outside Epcot near the bus stop. Nearly all of the restrooms at Epcot are out-of-date compared to the other park restrooms (who wants to manually flush at Walt Disney World?), but that one is particularly bad. It seems to be an afterthought of the cleaning crew.

Special prize for tiniest restroom open to the public: Chefs de France. A pretzel should be something you eat in Germany, not something you turn into in France.

Mousejunkie Commandments

Each park has its own details that require special planning. But there are a few blanket philosophies that will serve you well no matter where you are at Walt Disney World:

MOUSEJUNKIE WALT One of the least-used and spotless restrooms in all of Walt Disney World is in the Magic Kingdom, believe it or not. It's a well-kept secret, but I'll give you precise directions to it right now.

Head for Liberty Square—near the Hall of Presidents. There's a counter service restaurant called the Columbia Harbor House. On the second floor of that restaurant you will find the most immaculate bathroom—men's or women's—in all of Disney World. It's true. If you take the Keys to the Kingdom tour and get the right tour guide, he'll confirm it. It might take a little more effort to get there, but given how clean it is, it's well worth the trip.

Disney commandos are the Navy SEALs of family holidays: They have a firm, detailed plan of attack from which there can be no deviation. They remain focused on the mission of squeezing every possible attraction into a given time period, and quite often wear the shell-shocked look of a grizzled warrior by day's end. They move quickly and leave no trace behind.

Mousejunkie Deb's Best Tips

➤ **Bring ponchos.** It's Florida.

➤ **Wear sunscreen and stay hydrated.** I do neither, but my mother says to.

➤ **Wear comfortable shoes, and bring at least two pairs to alternate.** I wear a pedometer, and you walk four to five miles in a day of park touring.

➤ **Make dining reservations early.** If it's all about the food in your family, like ours, you don't want to miss out on a favorite, or on a suggested establishment.

➤ **Stop to smell the flowers.** Or look at the topiaries. Or find hidden Mickeys. Pay attention to the details.

➤ **Stay at a Disney resort.** It may be a bit more money, or maybe not with discounts. But you'll be much more immersed in the magic, will enjoy the convenience, and qualify for Extra Magic Hours (A.M. or P.M.).

➤ **Don't overbuy your park passes.** With a little planning, you can avoid extras that will cost you, like paying for the Park Hopper option when you may not need it, or adding days you won't need. If partway through your vacation you realize you need more, you can upgrade without penalty.

➤ **Enjoy the resort pools.** Waterparks are fun, but if your kids are very young, save the money and take advantage of the free resort pools. They don't know the difference, but your wallet will.

➤ **Don't rent a car.** I know some people like having their own wheels, but with complimentary Magical Express, the monorail, busses, ferries, water taxis, and Friendship launches, it's hard to justify the expense. We consider the Disney transportation part of the experience. Once in awhile, it could be a bad experience, but an experience nonetheless. And you won't meet other fellow Mousejunkies in the back seat of your rental car.

➤ **Take advantage of the complimentary package delivery service.** Who wants to lug those souvenir purchases around? If you or your kid loses it, you're outta luck. If Disney loses it, they'll replace it from their vast inventory.

MOUSEJUNKIE DEB   At first, we toured the parks commando. That's how we *became* Mousejunkies. I would argue that if you haven't done them commando, you're not a true Mousejunkie.

Once you've achieved the Mousejunkie plateau, at that point you can put away the park maps with the checkmarks, and just go with the flow. What do you feel like doing? What have you had enough of? What just doesn't turn you on any more? What do you need to do to get your fix? The World is your oyster.

The best way to avoid lines is to go during non-peak seasons. This suggestion of course sparks debates among parents on the ethics of pulling your children out of school. If you don't have children, or don't have ethics, don't go in February, April, July, Thanksgiving week, or Christmas vacation.

We're not early morning people, so the second recommendation is to go later in the day. Everyone seems to have the idea of going early to avoid the crowds. Maybe, but no one says go late to avoid the crowds. So if no one is suggesting it, less people are doing it, opening it wide open for us "later" folks. That's when families go back to the hotels for breaks and children's meltdowns force them out of the parks.

The only strategy that doesn't work for is Fastpasses, which during busy times on popular attractions can "sell out" earlier in the day. Fastpasses are a good strategy for the popular attractions. Get those when you first enter the parks, unless there's no line when you get there—in that case, hop on. It truly is a good system and saves you a lot of wait time.

MOUSEJUNKIE JENNA Always bring a pen and grab a map. Go through the list of attractions and circle your must-dos and put an X on the things you don't want to do. Before you get twenty feet from the turnstiles, figure out a starting point. It could be "I'm going to Adventureland first" or "We need to get a Fastpass for Soarin'" or "Good Lord, I need coffee." Your best plan of attack is always going to be some kind of continuous line, hitting your top picks along the way. Zigzagging across the park is almost always a bad idea because it leads to confusion, short tempers and sore feet.

Fastpass is the best thing, ever, but it's worth some planning and advanced knowledge to make it really work for you. Some of it is just common sense. For instance, if you're going to the Magic Kingdom on a Saturday in July, Splash Mountain is going to be the ride that runs out of Fastpasses first.

Sometimes, it's hard to predict what your Fastpass experience will be like. Here are two examples of Fastpass on the same ride at the same time of year, but different days of the week: Soarin' is a popular ride at Epcot that fills up fast and has limited seats per hour. In May 2006, I grabbed a Fastpass for Soarin' at about noon, rode the Living With the Land boat ride with a five-minute wait, had a leisurely lunch at nearby Sunshine Seasons, and joined the Fastpass return line because my return time was one hour after I picked up my Fastpass. In May 2007, I got to The Land at 1 P.M., found that there were no more Fastpasses available for the rest of the day, and waited in the stand-by line for an hour. The chief

(Continued on next page)

difference is that my 2006 Epcot visit was on a Monday, while my 2007 visit was on a Sunday.

The main thing is to be flexible. Is it more important to ride Test Track together or ride Test Track quickly? The single rider line can cut wait times short, but you will ride with strangers. How much are you dying to see Spectromagic or Wishes? Wait times are often shorter during parades and fireworks. Are you willing to annoy your friends and family by insisting on seeing every single thing and setting off on a forced march? Or would you rather that your travel buddies enjoy themselves so much that they want to come back to WDW again, and soon? One thing is sure—the more often you visit, the easier it is to plan.

Above all, open your eyes and ears. It's the small things that make Walt Disney World such an addictive place.

"The best part about all the parks, after you've done them all so often, isn't seeing Philharmagic again, or riding Tower of Terror again," Mousejunkie Deb offers. "Although they're fun, the best part is taking in all the theming details and nuances of the Imagineers. Disney World is a creative, innovative, marketing marvel. The entire operation is nothing less than impressive."

Mousejunkies Recreate

Mickey Who?

THERE MAY NOT BE A vacation spot on the planet with a higher concentration of children than Walt Disney World, but there may not be a better place to get away from them, either.

Scoff if you must, but the Mouse House has a full roster of offerings guaranteed to infuse a bit of relaxation away from the sticky-hands set. Travelers can spend an entire vacation—enjoying everything from spa treatments and golf to specialized tours and fine dining—while managing to avoid the traditional kiddie traps.

Walt Disney World's most picturesque assets, its lakes, rivers and canals, present a perfect opportunity to put some distance between you and the long lines.

When I arrived in Orlando in January of 2006, I didn't know who Sammy Duvall was. At around 10 A.M. one breezy, sunny winter morning, I found out.

Evidently he's the guy who facilitates crazy people's wishes. For example: parasailing. Sure, many people will tell you it's a relaxing ride that provides a great view of the surrounding area. But I've always been of the mind that flying should only occur in airplanes, and sometimes "floating" can suddenly turn into "plummeting."

This is why I promptly volunteered my wife when the opportunity arose to parasail across Walt Disney's Bay Lake.

She was game, so by mid-morning we were making our way toward the Sammy Duvall Watersports Centre behind the Contemporary Resort on Bay Lake. In reality, Sammy Duvall is a waterskiing world champion. I suppose I would've felt better if I found out he was a "keep people from falling out of the sky" world champion, but given Disney's track record, I trusted them with my bride.

Minutes later we were aboard a powerful-looking sport boat, Amy was strapped into a harness, and the parachute was beginning to fill with air as we shot across Bay Lake. Only the mate called for a full stop, because the parachute was inverted and needed to be turned over. This was fine with me, because—I'm not sure, but—I think having an upside down parachute might be a bad thing.

We had a little while to talk, so I checked in on Amy's state of mind.

"Are you nervous?" I asked.

"No," she said. "I'm strapped to a parachute, what can go wrong?"

"You could break loose and float down into the alligators and snakes in that swamp over there," I said.

She smirked and got ready to make like Tinker Bell.

A few minutes later everything was worked out, Amy was strapped in and the boat began to accelerate. With a big smile and a wave, she began to float upwards, tethered to the back of the boat by a substantial rope. Everything was going smoothly, until about a minute into the trip when a gust of wind knocked her back. Her feet shot up into the air and her head was pointing toward the surface of the water far below. Evidently she thought this was a riot, because I could hear her distant laughter as the wind died down and she righted herself.

Me? I was hundreds of feet below, wondering if I knew where our life insurance policy was. Still, everything went completely according to plan.

As she hit the 450-feet-above-the-water mark, a magnificent view of the Magic Kingdom, and all of surrounding Walt Disney World—all the way into downtown Orlando—began to unfold. The deep hum of the motorboat drifted away, only to be replaced by a calm silence. The ride actually did become a relaxing, smooth trip, and the rush of the ascent soon gave way to the placid reflection of looking out over beautiful central Florida. According to Amy, seagulls circled below her—indicative of just how high she was.

Despite the misguided worrying of someone firmly planted on the ground, these people knew exactly what they were doing and know how to keep it fun and safe.

Finding Nemo

As it turns out, Walt Disney World has a whole roster of water sports that guests can take advantage of. Among the most relaxing are the guided fishing excursions. As an avid angler in the northeast, I've always lusted after the idea

of going toe-to-toe with one of Florida's legendary largemouth bass. And if I could do it in the shadow of the Magic
Kingdom? Even better.

Our fishing guide, Tom Stocker, arrived at the dock
promptly at 10 A.M.—just in time to rescue our party of
would-be anglers from the scorching Florida sun. Passing
out complimentary cool drinks, Stocker pointed one of the
fleet's pontoon boats toward a stand of low-hanging cypress
trees just beyond the former Discovery Island. We geared up
and had our lines in the water in no time.

Within minutes of our drifting toward the back side of
the island, the bass began to bite. Live bait, fishing rods, and
lures are included in the $210 price. On this day it was live
bait that put fish in the boat. (If only temporarily. Disney
observes a strict catch-and-release policy.)

Guided fishing trips are offered several times daily, with
knowledgeable and experienced guides ushering parties of
as many as five people around one of the property's several lakes. Disney's waterways are teeming with largemouth
bass, all but guaranteeing a lively trip.

We started the morning on Bay Lake behind the
Contemporary Resort, and then moved to the Seven Seas
Lagoon directly in front of the Magic Kingdom. The fish hit
consistently, but not rapidly, as the sun climbed higher in
the sky. The heat of the day was chasing the fish deeper and
wearing on our tiny crew. Stocker was determined to change
that, so he ordered us to reel 'em up and get comfortable. He
throttled up and before too long we were riding a wake into
the docks near Fort Wilderness.

I swung my rod out over the side of the boat, opened the bail and let the bait drop straight down. A silvery flash caught my eye, and a millisecond later the tip of my rod dove for the water. For the next twenty minutes this is how it went: Drop the bait, hold still, reel in a slippery trophy.

By the end of our much-anticipated trip, we had boated a combined eighteen fish. None of them approached the "legendary Floridian bass" standard, but the quantity more than made up for that. The fish averaged two to three pounds, and showed plenty of life when hooked. These were strong, determined fish who were ready to fight—not lazy lunkers that had been caught, boated, and released enough to know everything was going to turn out fine.

TIP *For the experienced angler, the word from Stocker is this: For sheer numbers, request Bay Lake or the Seven Seas Lagoon—but for the real lunkers, book an excursion out of Downtown Disney.*

Since we had, in reality, been on the hunt for monster fish, we opted to book one more excursion, this time from Downtown Disney. When all was said and done, we accomplished our mission—but not exactly as I had anticipated.

When we pulled into the dock following a two-hour guided fishing tour along Walt Disney World's Sassagoula River that afternoon, I found myself both sunburned and humbled. Sure, we boated one of Florida's legendary huge largemouth bass, but when I say "we," I specifically mean "someone other than me."

But that's O.K., because when it was all over we had boated maybe twelve fish in total. The big one—and this was a big one—was hauled in by my wife, so I'm not bitter. If you can believe that.

We were picked up at the dock near the House of Blues at Downtown Disney around 10 A.M. Our guide immediately turned the boat 90 degrees and plunged us into the small maze of rivers that spider out among the nearby resorts.

The fish in question hit about thirty minutes after we had anchored just to the side of a footbridge bordering the Port Orleans resort. An Arkansas shiner tempted the fish from the bottom of a murky weed bed. The rod bent, the drag sang, and a splash that sounded like a dog jumping into the water alerted everyone that this was going to be a keeper. I watched the rod dance to the left and then to the right, and Amy's fist churning to get the fish closer to the boat.

A short time later John, our guide, thrust his net into the water and helped boat a very healthy five-plus pound largemouth bass. Amy, who rarely gets out fishing, had taken the monster of the day. And her husband, the fisherman, could only watch with a mix of pride and frustration.

Meanwhile, I took a few three-quarter pounders from my post at the back of the boat. Three-year-old Katie, meanwhile, hooked into a strong three-pounder. She held it high and named it "Floppy." I steamed. But again, since she is of my bloodline, I think that I get some kind of credit when the books were closed on this trip.

A little later, as the competitive edge began to get the better of me—and as Katie and Amy continued to haul in very healthy bass—I saw my line go tight and felt something taking the bait. I wasn't going to let this one go. I dropped the tip of the rod downward for a moment, and then launched it skyward to set the hook. Unfortunately I think all I got was its dental work and maybe part of a lip.

I traded fish stories with our guide John, a Philadelphia native who took up fishing at the age of three, as the sun started to turn my translucent Irish skin a painful pink.

The guides at Disney's fishing program know the miles of rivers and canals intimately, and while there are no guarantees in life, catching some nice bass on a fishing trip at Walt Disney world is all but a sure thing.

But, as a wise man once said, "That's why they call it 'fishing' and not 'catching.'"

TIP *When booking a fishing trip, make absolutely sure the cast member on the phone is crystal clear where and when you are to meet your guide.*

In three excursions booked on Disney's waterways, our guides failed to show up three times. They (or we) were either at the wrong location, they (or we) had booked the wrong time, or there was some other unexplained mix-up.

Frantic phone calls resulted in rebooking the trips, but it led to schedule changes and great consternation. To kill the time between when we were supposed to fish, and when we actually went fishing, we did a few loops around the Magic Kingdom area monorail whilst grumbling. At one point we pressed our noses against the window while looking forlornly at a family catching fish on the Seven Seas Lagoon below us. It was sheer torture, but in the end it worked out.

Cast members admitted that reservation process changes at the time had resulted in many mistakes. Here's to hoping time and practice has improved the odds of successful booking.

Winding Down

After a long morning on the water, guests can head to one of two spas located on Disney property: the spa at the Grand Floridian or Disney's Saratoga Springs Resort & Spa.

The spa at the Saratoga Springs resort is tucked into the middle of the sprawling vacation club project, just across the lake from Downtown Disney. Surrounded by the Victorian architecture that evokes the horse-racing influence of the spa's upstate New York namesake, visitors will find an instantly relaxing atmosphere.

The Grand Floridian spa is in its own separate lakeside building, a short walk from the resort.

Treatments range from the standard manicure/pedicure to the more interesting Adirondack Stone Therapy, in which heated stones and oils are used to loosen stress points and knots. With nary a youngster in sight, the searing heat and daunting queues at the Disney World attractions couldn't seem farther away.

MOUSEJUNKIE JENNA I took advantage of discounts offered to DVC members and booked a fifty-minute Swedish massage and a peppermint pedicure for the day I arrived at WDW. It seemed like an excellent way to dive into vacation relaxation.

Saratoga Springs is a very calm and quiet resort in the first place, but the spa there is so far removed from Mickey Mouse, popcorn, and Fastpasses that it's almost spooky. It's a place of barely audible instrumental music, cotton waffle-weave robes, and pitchers of ice water served in a lounge where everyone whispers. It's a very relaxing atmosphere, but not somewhere to get excited about a Disney trip.

My first appointment was the Swedish massage. My massage therapist asked me some questions about allergies and trouble spots, and went to work on all those airplane coach seat knots. I think fifty minutes is just enough massage to relax without feeling ridiculous, though the spa offers shorter and longer massage times. Unfortunately, I am a bit chatty, so I never took the opportunity to just tune out. Afterward, I had a ten-minute break in the lounge. It seems to me that it has some special name like Quiet Lounge or Meditation Room, which gives you a hint to its sole purpose. You are supposed to sit in this quiet room with its dimmed lights, drink ice water and not talk.

Soon, I was called by the technician who would be doing my pedicure, and fled the quiet room. I was for-

(Continued on next page)

tunate enough to travel to Walt Disney World while the spa at Saratoga Springs was offering its Peppermint Pedicure. The Peppermint Pedicure is named after a candy famous in Saratoga Springs (and sold in the Artist's Palette gift shop): the Peppermint Pig. The hand-and-foot treatment room has two pedicure chairs and two manicure tables. Additionally, they can set up a portable manicure station so guests getting a mani-pedi can get their fingers polished while their tootsies are soaking. The Peppermint Pedicure includes a soak in the foot spa, a massage with a tingly and fresh-smelling peppermint lotion, and the usual trim and polish. At fifty minutes, the pedicure lasted as long as the Swedish massage and I think I enjoyed it more. When I was done, my spa technician sent me off with all of the emory boards, buffing blocks, and toe separators she used on me, and tucked a nice-sized sample of the peppermint lotion for good measure.

It was a very relaxing visit to the spa, but I don't know that I can fully recommend it as a first-day treat. This was the second time that I have spent my first day at Walt Disney World at the spa. It was also the second time that I have left the spa worried that my luggage wouldn't be waiting in my new hotel room (it wasn't the first time) and that I'd show up late for dinner with massage oil in my hair and in the same tired clothes I flew down in.

If you want the relaxation of a spa visit to last, my advice is to schedule it in the middle of your vacation on a day when you have no concrete plans.

Fore at Five

MOUSEJUNKIE DEB Mention hitting the links at Walt Disney World and your first thought might be a carefree game of miniature golf. You'd be wrong—although they do have three of those courses, too. We're talking five professionally designed, PGA championship 18-hole courses and a 9-hole walking course whose design and course management strategy challenge the most avid golfers.

Water and other hazards abound throughout Disney's links, making for a tough but fun game on all the well-maintained greens. Golfers should take advantage of the four driving ranges and equally as many putting greens to limber themselves up for play. Each 18-hole Disney course earned an impressive 4.0-4.5 out of 5.0 rating from *Golf Digest*.

Bonnet Creek Golf Club was rated 4.5 by *Golf Digest*. Osprey Ridge and Eagle Pines offer four tees to play: Talon (professional), Crest (men), Wings (senior), and Feathers (women). Oak Trail, designed by Ron Garl, is a par 36 course designed for juniors and beginners.

Whimsical Yet Demanding

When players first enter Bonnet Creek and see the amusing Mickey Mouse golf cart parked at the clubhouse, for a moment you may think you'll be finishing up the course aiming for the clown—or Mickey's—nose for a free round. But as soon as you see the first hole

(Continued on next page)

beyond the starter, you realize you're in for a great day of demanding yet enjoyable play.

Architect Tom Fazio designed the picturesque Osprey Ridge course. This par 72 course offers a quiet, scenic game with many fun challenges, heavy on bunkers (seventy of them) and elevation changes, and generous width fairways that cut through various species of trees. One of Florida's most environmentally friendly golf courses, it contains eight nesting platforms atop tall poles for ospreys, alongside ponds stocked with the fish that ospreys eat. The course also features hand-built boardwalks, instead of asphalt or concrete cart paths, winding through its wetlands.

The Sand Trap Bar and Grill overlooks the picture-postcard eighteenth green of the Osprey Ridge golf course.

The Palm and Magnolia courses also share an entrance, clubhouse, and the like, each located near the Magic Kingdom. They also share the same course architect: Joe Lee. The Palm, named after the vegetation that has been strategically planted along the course, is the choice of many novices for its casual play, but this course contains 9 water holes and 94 bunkers, keeping veteran golfers coming back. The 18th hole has been rated as the fourth toughest hole on the PGA Tour. Its first 6 holes take you close to the Magic Kingdom, before heading away from the area.

The Magnolia course sports the famous Mickey Ears sand bunker (1 of 97 bunkers) on the par 3, 6th hole (a very large "hidden Mickey" for those who follow them), of which you can purchase an aerial photo in the pro shop. This course is Disney's longest, at 7,200 yards, and has a good amount of water. Over fifteen hundred magnolia trees grace its fairways. It's been the locale of the PGA Tour's FUNAI Classic for thirty-five years (now the Children's Miracle Network Classic), and each year hosts the final round of the PGA Tour's Disney Golf Classic at Walt Disney World Resort. This is your opportunity to play where the champions play. One of the game's most famous, Payne Stewart, holds the course record of 61. The back five holes run close to the Magic Kingdom.

The Lake Buena Vista course, designed by architect Joe Lee, unwinds through two Disney Vacation Club resorts: Old Key West and Saratoga Springs Resort and Spa, and is close to Downtown Disney. It's an extremely charming course to play, beautiful on a sunny Florida day. At 6,749 yards, it is the shortest of Disney's 18-hole offerings, and has narrower fairways than the other courses. An abundance of thick Bermuda grass rough adds to its obstacles. Interesting tidbit: The LBV course is one of a select few that have hosted a PGA Tour event, an LPGA Tour event, and a USGA event.

The Magnolia, Palm, and Lake Buena Vista courses all offer four tees to play from as well.

A Good Walk

If you haven't done enough walking in the theme parks, play a round at Oak Trail, Disney's 9-hole, 36 par walk-

(Continued on next page)

ing course designed by architect Ron Garl. It offers two tees—men's and women's, and was given a 3.5 rating from *Golf Digest*. This course is serene and secluded, and offers an opportunity to golf without the crowds that the other courses attract. Because it's a walking course, Oak Trail provides a leisurely pace and contest.

While many could argue that golf is golf, Disney Golf has a number of unique things associated with it:

> ➤ The starters will give you biodegradable cornstarch tees.

> ➤ In today's World of expensive vacation costs (yes that W is capitalized), Disney provides complimentary transportation between on-site hotels and any of their golf courses. The hotel will give you a voucher, which covers the cab fare and a gratuity.

> ➤ If you bring your own clubs, bell services will store them for you in a locked hotel facility at no cost if you're staying on property. Professional line rental clubs and shoes are available if you don't want to lug your clubs on vacation with all your suitcases of clothes, or home with all your bags of souvenirs.

> ➤ If you're playing at more than one course during your vacation, you can leave your clubs at one course, and then Disney will transfer your equipment to the next course.

> ➤ All courses practice water conservation, using reclaimed wastewater for irrigation.

> ➤ All five championship greens are certified by Audubon International as Cooperative Wildlife Sanctuaries.

➤ Disney Golf offers lessons and clinics. The ESPN Golf School's Junior Academy is hosted at the Palm/Magnolia facility.

➤ Mandatory golf carts are equipped with accurate GPS systems that track your pace, and the yardage of surrounding golfers. This feature not only provides a terrific safety tool, but also helps keep the pace of play at a comfortable level for everyone. The GPS system also tells you how far you are from the pin, helping you pick just the right club for your next shot.

TIP *This is Florida, so alligators are among the residents who call this state home. But starters also caution golfers, especially out-of-state players, about the water moccasins. So rather than looking for your ball near a swampy area, it's best to pull another out of your bag.*

Fees

Playing golf at these beautiful courses doesn't come cheap. During peak seasons, the top course can take $150+ bite out of your vacation budget. Disney does offer many discounts, including summer price slice, twilight rates, an active military discount, special resort guest pricing, annual passholder discounts, and annual membership card pricing. Eighteen holes of golf during fall's twilight special can be played for as little as $25, making the courses very affordable for those traveling

(Continued on next page)

off peak and willing to golf during off hours. Even Oak Trail offers twilight rates, as low as $10. And while all the 18-hole courses charge the same for all ages, Oak Trail offers junior pricing and free rental clubs for those under seventeen.

Individuals, as well as formal tournaments and informal scrambles, are welcome. Specialists will customize and coordinate for you, complete with gift and prize packages and food and beverage options.

For group outings, call 1-407-938-3870. For information and individual tee times, call 1-407-WDW-GOLF (4653). For more information, visit www.disneyworldgolf.com.

Worth Mentioning: Dinner without the Kids

There are literally scores of adult dining choices at Disney, but for the best views this side of Cinderella's Castle, head to the California Grill, located atop the Contemporary Hotel.

Guests also can enjoy an evening without the kids at Citricos at Disney's Grand Floridian Resort and Spa; Jiko—The Cooking Place at Disney's Animal Kingdom Lodge; Artist Point at Disney's Wilderness Lodge; Todd English's bluezoo at Walt Disney World Dolphin; and The Dining Room at Wolfgang Puck's in Downtown Disney.

Visitors wishing to truly upgrade their dining can opt to splurge at Victoria and Albert's at the Grand Floridian, a special-occasion restaurant designed to cater to the most discriminating culinary tastes. A customized seven-course gourmet meal is served each night in the intimate sixty-five-seat dining room. The wine cellar, with more than 700 selections on the menu and 4,200 in the cellar, has been recognized by *Wine Spectator* magazine with an Award of Excellence.

Of course, this being Disney, each waitress answers to Victoria, every waiter is known as Albert, and diners are presented with a personalized menu at the end of the meal. Dinner is $95 per person, $145 with a wine pairing. The coveted Chef's Table is $125 per person, $185 with a wine pairing.

Specialized Epcot Tour

Disney's theme parks also offer specialized tours that can put guests miles away from the crowds on the other side of the ropes. Visitors to Epcot, for instance, now can take a tour of the park's World Showcase hours before it opens to the general public astride a Segway Human Transporter.

The cost is $80 for a one-hour training session and a one-hour guided park tour.

Stepping onto a Segway for the first time is a bit like balancing a broom handle on the palm of one's hand and can take a bit of practice. Piloting it around a series of cones on an inside obstacle course of sorts provides a bit of confidence. Despite this preparation, several riders found themselves pitched off the machine on a recent tour—one flew forward after cutting a corner near a pillar in the America pavilion, another drove too close to a wall in Epcot's France and a third rammed his Segway into the side of a bridge near the International Gateway.

Despite these relatively minor mishaps, participants were enthusiastic about the tour. The machines are set at a maximum top speed of five miles per hour, and cast members are readily available to guide newbies through the experience. Only ten people at a time can participate, allowing visitors an exclusive look at the park as it awakens for the day.

Yes, there is a Walt Disney World for grownups where the crush of the theme parks becomes a distant memory, and it becomes possible to visit Disney World and never have one child smear its sticky hands on you.

Mousejunkies Procreate

I WAS ONCE A WALT DISNEY WORLD pro, jaunting from park to park, eating at all the best restaurants, never standing in line for anything, and laughing disdainfully at the shell-shocked, exhausted guests toting screaming, exhausted children behind them.

"Ha ha," I'd say, "let us enjoy a second Dole Whip while these folk berate their children into having fun."

And then we'd scamper off to some location—very likely air conditioned and very likely serving Yuengling.

And then one day I found myself at the gates of the Kingdom with my own toddler. How could this have happened? (Actually, I know exactly how it happened, but that's another story.)

I do know that it changed everything. Within the first thirty minutes at the Magic Kingdom with our child I thought I was on my way to being crippled. My back was weary, my three-year-old daughter was sporting a thousand-yard stare, my better half was berating the child about the need for sleep, and I swear my eyes were more sunken than they had been just a half an hour earlier.

But most shockingly, I had yet to visit Raglan Road, the Walt Disney World Resort's new Irish Pub.

We had become that which we once mocked.

Don't get me wrong, I'm not telling you to leave your kids at home when you visit Walt Disney World. Although until 2006 I had done just that thing on several occasions. All I'm saying is that once there's a kid in the mix, your Disney skill sets undergo a drastic change.

There is just more to think about with a youngster along for the ride. Transportation, strollers, diapers, making sure she gets a proper breakfast and stays hydrated and the omnipresent mood gauge are just a few of the new skills we had to learn when we first brought our daughter to Walt Disney World.

Just getting from one side of the park to another was a new experience. I was bound and determined not to let it get the best of me, however. I was a Disney pro, and bringing along a single child would not bring me to my knees.

Tackling the Magic Kingdom

The Magic Kingdom is the Holy Grail for the younger set. It is the iconic park and it has the most attractions appropriate for children.

It's also where I had my Disney ego crushed.

On previous trips I went where I wanted, when I wanted. Once we had a youngster in tow, we had to judge how she might deal with almost every aspect of park touring. The Many Adventures of Winnie the Pooh may seem tame to an enthusiastic and admittedly geeky newspaper editor, but to a three-year-old it's not necessarily all honey and Heffalumps.

In fact, it was the Heffalumps in particular that scared her. And the ominous thunder cracks that signified that the rain, rain, rain was about to come down, down, down didn't help. It all started out fine, but about halfway through plaintive cries of "I don't like this" began to emanate from the front of the honey pot that was whirling us through the Hundred Acre Wood.

TIP *If your child shows fear or starts to cry while in line at an attraction, consider skipping it. It's not worth the frustration involved as you attempt to calm an upset child while adding up the cost of the trip in your head.*

A friend related a similar experience to me just days before we arrived. He said he brought his son on an attraction despite signs of nervousness. For the rest of the trip his son didn't want to go on *any* attractions. I took his advice to heart, but didn't put it into practice.

Looking back, I couldn't have foreseen it. She liked Dumbo and Cinderella's Golden Carousel. We then made our way to The Many Adventures of Winnie the Pooh. It's a very mild, happy attraction designed for young kids. I didn't give it a second thought. After a bit of a wait you get into a cart and it shuttles you through a set of doors and into the dark.

It started out fine, but a little ways in we hit the aforementioned Heffalumps and Woozles and everything went south quickly.

I always saw the attraction as a nostalgic tour of A. A. Milne's whimsical tales. But she didn't see it that way. She saw it as monsters followed by a violent storm. She carried the scars of that trauma for years, refusing to set foot in the Hundred Acre Wood. What did I learn? Sometimes it's O.K. to let the kid decide. It makes for a smoother trip.

What had once been a childhood friend was now seen as the enemy. And once Winnie the Pooh was the bad guy, we knew we would have to move forward cautiously and with great forethought.

TIP *If it's not too hot, have your toddler or child wear his or her bathing suit underneath their clothes. The Magic Kingdom and Epcot both have fountains where kids can play and get wet.* **Pooh's Playful Spot** *(in Fantasyland in the Magic Kingdom) is a good place to sit back and relax while your child romps through the fountains, slides, and furnished tree house.*

In the process of frightening our child, we did learn to keep a close eye on her mood and reaction to the first attraction or two. Doing so can gauge just how the rest of the day—and possibly the rest of the trip—will go.

By this point in the trip it had become painfully clear: Our theme park approach had changed dramatically and for the foreseeable future. Caution and forethought—outside of planning a few dinners and recreation options—were never part of our Disney strategy.

A three-year-old rates several Magic Kingdom attractions:

➤ **Mad Tea Party**—"I liked the tea cups. They spin around."

➤ **The Many Adventures of Winnie the Pooh**—"I'm scared of that ride because I'm the littlest kid in my class." (I don't understand that explanation, either.)

➤ **Carousel of Progress**—"Mama doesn't like this, but I do. It was fun because there was lots of shows on it."

➤ **Dumbo the Flying Elephant**—"I like this ride because we get to fly."

➤ **Toon Town**—"Can we go on Dumbo again?"

➤ **Tomorrowland Speedway**—"I like these slow cars because I drive."

➤ **The Haunted Mansion**—"(Unintelligble crying) Dumbo... Mumble... (More crying.)"

➤ **Tomorrowland Transit Authority**—"I thought it was going to be scary, but it was fun."

➤ **The Magic Carpets of Aladdin**—"Jasmine is my favorite. The camels make faces like this (makes a face like the camel)."

➤ **Enchanted Tiki Room**—"I like that song."

➤ **Pirates of the Caribbean**—"This is too scary for me."

➤ **It's a Small World**—"No! No! No! No!"

➤ **Country Bear Jamboree**—"Big Al looks like you, Daddy."

➤ **Cinderella's Golden Carousel**—"I got to ride Cinderella's horse. I want to do it again."

For most youngsters, each of these attractions should be fine.

★ **TIP** *When it comes to character encounters, be patient. See how your child reacts the first time they see a character. If they* *act frightened, don't force it. Our little one was a little nervous as we were approaching Mickey in the Judge's Tent in Toontown, but the look of sheer joy on her face when she finally came around the corner and saw him was worth the gamble.*

Rules to Relax By

With a child in tow you've got to plan on a little crankiness. It's usually hot, crowded, and you can be up early and out until very late. It's not an excuse for a child to misbehave, but for a young kid a schedule like that can be taxing. Heck, for a forty-year-old it can be taxing.

I still won't tolerate our child freaking out. But I think a certain amount of crankiness has to be expected. It's hard, because a Walt Disney World vacation isn't the cheapest way to spend a week and there are very high expectations. But on every trip I see far too many parents trying to berate their kids into having fun, which almost always results in a general meltdown.

TIP *Midday naps can be valuable. That is, if your kid will nap. Ours usually won't, but a little down time can help. It certainly helps her mother, I'll tell you that. Plus, it gives me time to watch Stacey on the in-room resort TV channel.*

No matter where guests stay on-property, from the most exclusive suite at the Grand Floridian Resort to the most affordable studio at Pop Century, there is one element that unites them all, and that is Stacey Aswad.

Aswad is the super-friendly, ultra-perky host that guides viewers through the Disney parks on its in-room resort infor-

MOUSEJUNKIE WALT You might want to test the whole character thing before you ruin an expensive character meal. I was at a character meal at the Liberty Tree Tavern with my niece, two, and nephew, four. Chip and Dale and Miko came to our table, and the kids freaked out. They were very afraid of the characters. A few minutes later Minnie Mouse came over and they had no fear at all. She totally calmed them. What I found is that it's not the person in this big-headed character suit as much as familiarity. They weren't afraid of Mickey or Minnie at all, but an innocent looking Miko came over and they lost it.

mation channels. Love her or hate her, there's no escaping her high-energy welcome. Turn on the TV in any Disney resort, and there she is—colorful, cute, enthusiastic, and ultimately helpful. She runs through a "top seven" list of attractions and sprinkles helpful tips throughout.

There are two guarantees on every Walt Disney World trip: I will start and end each day by watching Stacey for a while, and Amy will roll her eyes every time I do it.

The next thing we learned is not to base your vacation around Disney's colorful and conveniently available characters. They certainly are part of the Walt Disney World experience, but standing in line for any amount of time to get a picture with a character is not an efficient use of time.

Sure, the character pictures are nice and our child really likes to meet her favorites, but it's not worth the time that it can take or the chaos it sometimes causes. Not everyone abides by social rules such as "waiting your turn" or "standing in line" or "not running you over to get to Pluto." I've never thought it was worth any amount of aggravation. And after a while, it all starts to blend in. After the twelfth character greeting on our first trip with our daughter I have a vivid memory of asking my wife: "How many pictures like this do we really need?"

I put more value in photos of her reactions to unexpected events or resting in her mother's arms after a long day. If you still feel like you need your character interaction, let them come to you.

TIP *Book a couple of character meals. The characters come to you. It's much easier and it all takes place inside—so it's air conditioned. Plus, food.*

Strollers Are Your Friend

If your child will still fit in a stroller, bring it. You can pack your own or rent one at the parks. We brought our own, and I'm very happy we did. While it is a pain to get it on and off the Disney buses, it looks different from the vast fleet of rental strollers that converge in alarming numbers in Fantasyland, and is therefore easier to find after exiting an attraction.

TIP *Having your stroller stolen is a hazard every parent must face, but here's a unique strategy that may lessen the* *chances of this happening. It's simple: Take a diaper, put it in a see-through freezer bag, pour some root beer into the bag and hang it from your stroller's handle. Voila—the "soiled diaper gambit" keeps your property safer from stroller poachers.*

Granted, people may ask why the heck you'd hold on to a dirty diaper when there are trash cans every six feet, but it's bound to scare off the morally challenged visitors skulking the byways of the Magic Kingdom.

It's also more common for the Disney rental strollers to be stolen. You can't tell them apart, so it'd be hard to identify it as yours.

I get totally wiped out walking around all day, so the last thing I want to do is carry my daughter around all night. Putting her in the stroller conserves her energy, it helps us keep track of where she is all the time, and it gives us a place to put stuff—cameras, souvenirs, and so forth. Not to mention it preserves her dad's back for a few more years

TIP *Mark your stroller with something that's easy to spot. It makes it much easier to locate after riding an attraction, especially if it was moved from where you parked it on the way in.*

On a related note, be on your best behavior when it comes to dealing with the cast members in the parks. They work hard to put on a great show, and they're standing in the same heat and humidity you are. (Despite urban myths to the contrary, there are no wearable air conditioners that keep them cool inside those bulky, uncomfortable costumes and uniforms.) They're quite often underappreciated and overworked, and they always tend to bear the brunt of grumpy guests' frustrations.

Why bring this up now? Cast members have clued me in to specific instances when guests were less than civil and how they dealt with it. Cast members, while helpful, skilled, and committed to making your vacation a great one, are also in charge of moving your stroller when you're inside an attraction if necessary. While you're sitting in an air-conditioned theater watching Mickey's Philharmagic, the cast member you just lambasted about standby wait times is outside in the 98-degree heat escorting your stroller to Jacksonville.

TIP *Use the "baby swap" to experience any attractions you might want to, but your child does not (or is too short for). It works like this: Parents and child queue up together. Parent A rides first, while parent B stands to one side with the child. Once the ride is over, the parents trade places and parent B gets to ride the attraction without waiting through the entire line again.*

Epcot with Kids

At first glance, Epcot has less to offer the little ones than the Magic Kingdom—what with the learning and lectures and such. Beyond the initial impression, however, there lies a full day of things to do for parents and children.

Here's what we've found works best when touring Epcot with youngsters:

Arrive at the park before it opens. When the ropes drop and everyone makes a mad-dash to get their Fastpass for Soarin', head straight for the **Character Connection** (located near the Fountainview Café) for some (normally) easy access to characters.

Innoventions East and West, which bookend Innoventions Plaza, have a number of playground style areas and activity areas where kids can color and create different projects.

These activity areas—**Kidcot Fun Stops**—are designated on park maps with a big "K" in a red square. There are sixteen of them located throughout Futureworld and the World Showcase. Children are given a cutout mask which they can color and decorate as they stop at each of the locations throughout the park. Cast members will also stamp the mask at each country or Kidcot Fun Stop.

The Kidcot Fun Stops are free, and if you don't point it out, they may not notice that they can also be educational. Kidcot Fun Stops are located in The Land, Test Track, Innoventions East and West, and The Seas With Nemo and Friends.

TIP *Be sure to check out the Epcot tip board in Innoventions Plaza. It provides updates on the standby wait times for several of the biggest attractions and can help you plan your day.*

The Living Seas With Nemo and Friends is a natural when traveling with children, and getting there is half the fun. After winding through an imaginatively designed queue area, guests board appropriately themed "clam mobiles" where they'll travel along a track to catch up with Nemo—who has wandered off again—by traveling through a coral reef populated by actual denizens of the deep. Visitors glide by displays that use new animation techniques which project characters from the film into tanks of actual aquatic creatures.

Headlining the pavilion proper is the interactive **Turtle Talk With Crush**. Crush, the stoner/surfer character from *Finding Nemo* treats guests to ten-minute shows where he interacts with, talks to, and messes with the audience. No two shows are alike, and it's a clever, customized attraction perfect for kids.

The complex is tucked into a series of tanks that make up a 5.7-million-gallon marine environment—one of the largest of its kind anywhere.

Futureworld is home to the 3-D movie, ***Honey, I Shrunk the Audience***. Based on the *Honey I Shrunk the Kids* film series, this attraction may alternately entertain your youngsters or cause them to run shrieking from the theater. It can be loud and it features a huge 3-D snake. It also takes advantage of tactile surprises that can startle easily spooked little ones. Other than that, it's based on a film that came out in 1989, which leaves it a bit dated in terms of pop culture.

Next door is the **Imagination** pavilion, home to **Journey Into Your Imagination**. I've thus far avoided taking my daughter on it, only because it is awful. It's gone through three reboots over the years, each one more revolting than the next. The changes made over the course of two redesigns in the span of a few short years were rather extreme. It may have been time to oust the Dreamfinder—the attraction's original host—but when Disney unveiled the results of the rehab, guests were less than enthusiastic. It was clinical, lacked heart, and failed to connect with guests.

Imagineers were ordered to shut it down and launch a do-over. Again, it opened to deafening ambivalence.

Originally the attraction featured Figment, a small purple dragon, and his creepy friend, the Dreamfinder. (Creepy is my description entirely. Others found him to be whimsical and delightful. I am suspicious of those people.) Together, Dreamfinder and Figment sang songs and showed guests how to use their imagination. This was changed completely when Eric Idle of Monty Python's Flying Circus was cast as Dr. Nigel Channing, who hosted the attraction after a major rehab in 1999.

"You don't have to be hit over the head with a hammer to express imagination," Mousejunkie Randy said of the revamp. "The original attraction had something magical about it. They completely gutted it when they re-did it."

When a new attraction opens at a Disney theme park, it is usually met with long lines for months afterward. We visited the newly re-opened Journey Into Your Imagination in 1999 and found it to be completely devoid of visitors. It remained a walk-on until it was shut down for a rehab only two years later.

Now, it still features Idle as Channing, but the storyline has been changed and Figment is back in more than a cameo role. It remains one of the weaker attractions at Disney World, but it's not entirely a waste of park time. If there isn't a line (Who am I kidding? There won't be a line) and it's threatening to rain, head on inside. As long as your child isn't afraid of the dark, it can be mildly entertaining.

The **Image Works playground** at the end of the attraction offers a number of interactive activities that parents can play with alongside their children. Visitors can send free e-mail postcards home from the post-attraction play area. The jumping fountains outside this pavilion also offer a great spot for a breather.

TIP *Kids get a kick out of the IBM Internet Postcards, located in Innoventions West. It allows families to take a picture of themselves and then send it via e-mail to friends back home. The postcards are available in several languages.*

The **World Showcase** hosts eleven **Kidcot Fun Stops**— one in each country. The activity areas are staffed by cast members native to the specific country, who will stamp the child's mask and quite often write something in their native language.

Kids can also purchase an Epcot passport, which cast members will stamp at each country.

The World Showcase has several experiences that target youngsters. A **hedge maze** in the United Kingdom is just the right size for younger children. Kids can join the **fife and drum corps** outside the American Experience as they recite the Pledge of Allegiance. A **miniature train display** next to the Germany pavilion can keep kids entertained for a few minutes. A stand of **hand drums** at the African village

is very likely to keep youngsters attention for a bit longer.
They can bang away for as long as they like, dancing and
making as much noise as they like.

Strollers in the Studios

Disney's Hollywood Studios is the home of **Playhouse
Disney Live!** That, alone, is enough of a reason to point the
stroller at this theme park and begin marching.

Characters from a number of The Disney Channel's
shows take the stage live, in a singing, dancing and storytell-
ing performance that urges the tykes to get up and take part.
The show is geared toward preschool-aged audiences, and is
located in the Animation Courtyard.

Stage shows are among the best options when you've
got kids along for the day at the Studios. **Beauty and the
Beast**, located on Sunset Boulevard just before the Twilight
Zone Tower of Terror, is a Broadway-style spectacle not
to be missed. Sadly, pre-show performances by Four For a
Dollar—an a cappella group tasked with warming up the crowd
and an audience favorite for years—has been discontinued.

Voyage of the Little Mermaid combines live actors, animation, laser displays and some incredibly innovative
puppeteers to tell Ariel's story. This seventeen-min-
ute production often draws crowds, but the theater
can hold a substantial number of people so the wait
time (the queue is covered, protecting little ones
from direct sun and rain) tends to be reasonable.

If there's a wait at **Muppet Vision 3-D**, consider
yourself lucky. The pre-show contains dozens of puns

and jokes—particular to the Muppets' sense of humor—that will entertain parents, and keep youngsters occupied.

The show is very similar in execution to Mickey's Philharmagic in the Magic Kingdom, and It's Tough to be a Bug in Disney's Animal Kingdom. Where Bug might frighten children, Muppet Vision 3-D is mild and funny enough to keep everyone in the family happy.

Disney's Imagineers are constantly pushing the envelope, coming up with inventive ways to entertain guests, and using the latest technologies to wow visitors. So what do younger kids find the most fun? Water fountains and playgrounds. Just like the ones they could've played at down the street for a lot less money and effort. Regardless, the **Honey, I Shrunk the Kids Movie Adventure Set** remains great fun.

Kids can crawl around on oversized props from the film, including giant ant hills, oversized blades of grass, huge bugs and a monstrous sneezing dog nose.

For slightly older kids, the **Great Movie Ride** can be fun. It's in the reproduction of Mann's Chinese Theater at the end of Hollywood Boulevard. (Walk toward the Sorcerer Mickey hat and keep going.) Just because there aren't any people waiting outside the theater doesn't mean a queue hasn't formed. This attraction can hold a great many people inside.

The twenty-minute guided tour through movie history is entertaining, but easily-spooked youngsters may find the *Alien* portion of the attraction a bit unsettling.

Animal Kingdom with Kids

At one time considered a half-day theme park by experienced vacationers, Disney's Animal Kingdom has expanded during its ten years of existence. Thrill rides, learning experiences, and stage shows now make this park a must-do for anyone spending time at Walt Disney World. Activities for children abound.

The **Festival of the Lion King** is, hands down, the single best stage show on Disney property, and appropriate for all ages. A Broadway-caliber show based on the film, this production features live singing performances, acrobatic displays, wire acts, dancing and audience participation.

TIP *Try to sit as close to the front as possible if you bring a child to Festival of the Lion King. Near the end of the performance, cast members pull children up from the audience to take part in the finale.*

By comparison, **Finding Nemo: The Musical** seems a bit anticlimactic. But just a bit. Brightly costumed cast members manipulate puppets across a massive stage. The music is catchy and the cast of characters is extensive. This performance is fine for all ages, but may do best with younger children.

The gate buster at Disney's Animal Kingdom is certainly **Kilimanjaro Safaris**. Guests board a large safari truck and are taken on a guided tour of a 100-acre east African savanna that serves as home to dozens of species of animals. Guests have a chance to catch an extreme close-up view of elephants, giraffes, antelope, lions, hippos, cheetahs, and rhinos, among other beasts.

In light of the breathtaking encounters with live animals, a storyline involving poachers seems almost an afterthought. This nearly twenty-minute ride through a small re-creation of Africa is an enthralling experience for all ages.

Youngsters can spend hours playing in the **Boneyard**, and meeting Disney characters at the various **character greeting trails**.

On my first trip to Walt Disney World as an adult, I was caught in a downpour while walking through Disney's Animal Kingdom. Seeking some kind of cover, we scurried by the **Flights of Wonder** theater. It was suggested we go inside and catch the show and perhaps get out of the rain.

My memorable response was, "I don't want to see a stupid bird show."

That phrase would be revisited upon me scores of times on every trip to Disney World since. It has become a "can't miss" event on our trips to Animal Kingdom, and without exception I am the one leading the charge to the theater.

A stage show featuring trained birds, it would be easy to pass this off as a simple parrot showcase. But deeper conservation themes, surprisingly funny cast members, and breathtaking stunts by trained hawks, cranes, owls, and other fowl make this show one of the strongest in the entire park.

Youngsters love the up-close encounters and their parents will enjoy the quick-witted host, Guano Joe.

While there are plenty of activities and attractions that parents and children can take part in together, there are a few the skittish should avoid. Obviously, the more thrilling attractions like Expedition Everest would not be a wise choice for little ones. But there is one attraction that draws kids like flies (you'll get that clever turn of phrase in a moment) and one parents should think twice about.

TIP *Avoid taking easily-scared tykes to see It's Tough to be a Bug—a 3-D experience located inside the lower portion of the Tree of Life. While the 3-D bug glasses may seem silly, the show always seems to frighten youngsters in the audience.*

Every performance of **It's Tough to be a Bug** I've attended has resulted in at least one absolute freak-out by a startled child. Large spiders descend from the ceiling, and several tactile surprises jar little ones unexpectedly. However, older children may love the show.

The first trip I took to Walt Disney World with my then three-year-old in tow was an unexpected wake-up call. It ended successfully, but it was a valuable learning experience upon which we based future trips.

Mousejunkies at Sea

The Tiny Ship Was Tossed

I HAD A SCREAMING HEADACHE, my stomach was threatening to disgorge itself of its contents, and my knees felt as if they were made of rubber. I opened my eyes slowly to see the face of Robin Williams staring back at me for what seemed like the nineteenth time in the last twenty-four hours.

Suddenly I could relate to Ernest Borgnine's character in *The Poseidon Adventure*.

I was sick as a dog and rather angry that I was spending my time aboard the *Disney Wonder*—the company's newest, most luxurious and finely appointed cruise ship—confined to our cabin. The movie *Patch Adams* played on a loop on our in-room TV. And the ocean just outside our window buffeted the ship as it lunged unevenly through the Atlantic.

We were sailing somewhere between Nassau and the southern tip of Florida aboard the *Disney Wonder* in the midst of Hurricane Irene. Any shore excursions had been cancelled—which was rather moot since we could not actually make landfall—and the captain decided we'd be safest riding the storm out at sea. The crew advised passengers to

stay inside and avoid the upper decks due to the rough con-
ditions. I contemplated this as I lay in our cabin, my body
wracked by some Bahamian Voodoo Curse Sickness.

In October of 1999 we had been offered a fairly good deal
to go on a cruise aboard the *Disney
Wonder*—one of the two cruise
ships that made up Disney Cruise
Lines at that time.

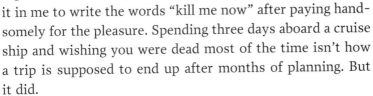

I tried to keep a travelogue during our cruise, but I just didn't have
it in me to write the words "kill me now" after paying hand-
somely for the pleasure. Spending three days aboard a cruise
ship and wishing you were dead most of the time isn't how
a trip is supposed to end up after months of planning. But
it did.

Experienced cruisers or sharp-eyed readers might have
picked up a key phrase just above: "In *October* of 1999."

October is hurricane season. It's also Idiots Cruise season.
And October of 1999 was an active Idiots Cruise season.

Prior to the cruise portion of our vacation, we spent four
bucolic days at Walt Disney World. We were staying at what
was then known as the Dixie Landings Resort. Dixie Landings
opened in 1992. It was divided into two sections: Alligator
Bayou—rustic log-style lodges—and Magnolia Bend—built
to resemble southern plantation grand manors. We spent
our days visiting parks with no lines, eating at wonderful
restaurants and having a great time. Our nights were restful
and rejuvenating, ensconced in the resort's Magnolia Bend
section.

After returning to our room one night, we saw a news report that featured a weather alert. The volume was turned down, but the meteorologist was pointing to an unmistakable shape: a swirling mass of clouds just southeast of Cuba.

This was the night before we were to head for Port Canaveral and board Disney's newest cruise ship. Watching the man on the TV point out the projected course of said swirl, I knew we were in for a rocky few days. But with our freight paid and Disney dictating our itinerary, we had no choice but to head for the coast, hold on tight, and make the best of things.

TIP *Hurricane season traditionally means better deals on cruise ship vacations—Disney or otherwise. But it's a roll of the dice. You could make it through unscathed, eating well and relaxing aboard a wonderful ship. Or, you could sail directly in the jaws of something approximating Hurricane Irene and swear off sea travel forever. The Mousejunkies' advice: Spring for peace of mind and avoid hurricane season.*

The *Wonder* was brand new, and had only traveled its Florida-to-the Caribbean route a handful of times. The schedule had us departing Port Canaveral late in the afternoon, arriving at Nassau early the next morning, leaving for the Disney-owned Castaway Cay in the middle of the next night, spending a day at sea and then landing back at home base.

In theory.

Irene had yet to impose her will on these well-laid plans. And what Irene wanted, Irene was going to get.

We rode a Disney Cruise Lines bus to the port, checked in, and boarded the sparkling, beautiful ship all within an hour or so. The *Disney Wonder* was the largest cruise ship in the area. Our room was much bigger and nicer than I ever imagined it would be, with a living room area, a bedroom area, two bathrooms and a very large porthole that measured about four feet across.

We attended the safety drill, and then headed up to the launch party. As we stood on the top deck, dark and foreboding clouds gathered in the distance. We consumed a few drinks, waved goodbye to people on shore, and began our trip through the canal and out to sea.

That night we had dinner together, met our server—Gordon, from Scotland—and decided to go see the film, *Mystery Alaska*, in the ship's movie theater. This was good, because watching the movie took our minds off the increasingly violent seas now rocking the ship. The water level in our glasses at dinner gave away what was going on in the darkness outside. The waters on top of which we were now steaming were becoming more and more tossed. The outer edges of Hurricane Irene were arriving.

As we lay in our bed later, the hangers in the closet clanged back and forth and the sliding door on our closet slammed open and shut as the ship was tossed left and right all night long. I was beginning to feel a bit out of sorts.

The next morning we awoke to see Nassau pulling into view. It was dark, raining, and gray. Every land and sea excursion had been canceled due to inclement weather, which left everyone to their own devices. There would be no wildlife tours, no sailing over to the other side of the island, and no visiting the Atlantis resort just across the bay.

We headed into town to do some shopping, but soon abandoned that plan when we found that Nassau's merchants primarily sold cheap t-shirts. We also encountered a knife-wielding group of locals that we opted to steer clear of. The group of eight to ten walked shoulder-to-shoulder across the middle of the street, forcing tourists to hoof it out of the way. One held a knife he continuously opened and closed to rather menacing effect. We were behind them when we noticed what was happening, so we ducked into a shop to let them get a little farther away.

An earlier hurricane had just come through just days before, and the port was left with some noticeable damage. Roofs were scarred, trees were uprooted, and sand covered every street. Between the surly locals and the damaged structures, we very quickly had enough of Nassau.

Before too long we were back on the ship.

We grabbed some drinks and hit the hot tub just as the lightning began to move in. I didn't mind, really, so we just quaffed our drinks and sat in the hot tub as the cold rain began to pound down on us. It was the best we could hope for, and being struck by lightning while holding a Mai Tai wasn't necessarily the worst fate that could've befallen us at that point.

A few hours later I would've welcomed the sweet embrace of oblivion.

To make up for the canceled excursions, the captain ordered servers to begin a two-for-one drink policy. By now I was feeling a bit less than normal, so I thought double-fisting drinks would make me forget what was ailing me. Turns out that wasn't such a good idea. Instead of being miserable, I was tipsy and miserable.

That night we did watch the live theater entertainment, which was great aside from watching it cross-eyed and ill, and then headed off to dinner at the Animator's Palate. Since we were in port and not moving at all, this was the best night of the cruise. The restaurant's décor starts out entirely in black and white, and ends with a flourish of color that imbues everything around with new life. It was a fantastic show and easily the high point of the entire cruise.

We returned to our room to find a wedding anniversary cake left for us by the crew. We didn't have any utensils, so we took a few messy samples and then crashed out for the rest of the night. I was looking forward to reaching Castaway Cay and getting off the ship for a few hours. During the night the ship began sailing toward the next stop on our itinerary, so the rocking and churning began anew.

The next day we awoke to see the camera mounted on the front of the ship, which was beamed to our in-room TV, pointing to an island. The caption at the bottom of the image said "Castaway Cay, four miles."

"Great," I thought. "We're almost there."

Amy and I got ready, and then I sat on the couch to watch us pull in to the island on the TV. Only the caption read, "Castaway Cay, nine miles."

We were going the wrong way. We were heading back out to sea—back out to the waves and the sickness where there would be nothing to do but become increasingly and sharply aware of the epidemic that was now sweeping through the ship. Someone had to tell the captain that somehow the ship had slipped into reverse.

Only seconds later we were given the announcement that because of the bad weather, today would be a "day at sea." For me, however, this would be "a day on as many seasick pills as I could get my hands on" and "a day in bed watching *Patch Adams* fifteen times while I tried to become unconscious."

One of the side effects of this twenty-four-hour period is that I now hate Robin Williams. He's probably a nice enough guy, and he's made some good movies. *Patch Adams* might even be among them, but having *any* movie play on a constant loop while battling the mysterious Bahamian Voodoo Curse Sickness would drive most people to acts of violence.

Whatever virus/bug/illness/voodoo curse sickness I caught, it had now fully set in. I was sick as a dog and didn't move for the rest of the day. It would be easy to diagnose the malady as seasickness, but I don't think that was the case. Years of recreational fishing off the New England coast made me familiar with the queasy feeling associated with bobbing in a boat in the North Atlantic. This was an entirely new experience. I believe it may have been an offshoot of Ebola with a dose of near-death thrown in and a bird-flu chaser. All I know is that I was looking for a light to walk into.

Instead, all I got was Robin Williams in a clown nose looking back at me approximately every two hours. The thought crossed my mind to get up and shut the TV off, thus ending the endless loop, but that would've meant actually standing—which I didn't feel quite up to at that point.

Amy took the video camera up to record the now nearly thirty-foot seas that were assaulting the ship, and tried to make the best of things.

I have very little memory of that night, except that I refused to stay in our cabin and miss a meal since we had already paid for everything. I dragged myself to the dining room, sat with my head in my hands and prayed for death. I didn't eat, but I felt I had achieved a small victory by at least taking my assigned, and paid for, seat at the table. I wasn't about to let something as inconsequential as an incapacitating illness in the middle of a full-on hurricane keep me down.

The upper decks were locked shut and everyone was ordered to stay inside. Things only got worse. One blurry day, a night filled with blackouts and a difficult packing process later, we were back at Port Canaveral. We boarded a bus, got back to the airport and arrived home a few hours later.

It took a few days to get our land legs back. Amy and I vowed we would never set foot on a cruise ship of any kind again. I understand Disney had nothing to do with this, and there was nothing they could have done to prevent it. But given the severity of my illness and the associated inconveniences, we will not be attempting it again.

But not everyone's Disney Cruise Line experience is quite as storm-tossed as ours was. The difference is noticeable from the outset. While cruising out to sea, the ships serenade passengers and bystanders along the shore with a cacophonous seven-note rendition of "When You Wish Upon a Star."

Cruisejunkies

From there, passengers are treated with much of the same attention to detail they've become accustomed to at Disney's land-based resorts.

The ships—the *Magic* and the *Wonder*—were designed specifically to host families. This means that while there are plenty of activities for the youngsters onboard, there's also an endless selection of activities for adults. That list just won't include gambling at the casino. Unlike most cruise ships, the *Magic* and the *Wonder* do not have an onboard casino. During my time aboard, I found it just as easy to inhale a tequila shooter and then throw my wallet overboard. It's pretty much the same experience.

There are ways to maximize your cruise experience, even if your family is traveling on a budget. It's a matter of knowing the secrets—and this being Disney, there is no shortage of unexpected bonuses.

It's no secret that an inside stateroom costs less to book. There is no porthole and no natural light. However, there are six staterooms located on the outside of the ship that are booked as "inside" staterooms. These "secret porthole rooms" are located on Deck Five and feature obstructed view portholes. Safety equipment blocks part of the view, but natural light (and possibly a safety light attached to the equipment outside) will flood your stateroom throughout the trip.

 **MOUSEJUNKIE RANDY** The consistency of the high level of service comes from the way Disney trains its staff. It doesn't matter if it's someone working at the Magic Kingdom or the person serving you drinks on the deck of a Disney cruise ship—it all starts at the top. The way they call the staff 'cast members' is a tip off—it's all about show, service and how you treat your guests.

If a bright, airy stateroom is on your list of "musts," the "secret porthole rooms" may be an economic way to get the best of both worlds.

TIP *The "secret porthole rooms" can be requested, but they go quickly so book as early as possible. They are rooms 5520, 5522, 5524 (almost completely blocked), 5020, 5022, 5024 (almost completely blocked).*

The "secret verandah rooms" offer slightly obstructed view verandahs for slightly less money. They're located at the back of the ship, where an overhang blocks part of the view.

TIP *Ask for cabins 6134, 6634, 7120, and 7620—the "secret verandah rooms" for a cabin with a slightly less expensive verandah.*

Those plans should include dinner at Palo. An elegant, adults-only restaurant serving northern Italian specialties, Palo is the only restaurant that requires reservations. An

MOUSEJUNKIE RANDY Like most cruise lines, you can book all your reservations online now. But since we're dealing with Disney, you can expect them to go the extra mile. For example: If you are traveling with a group of people under multiple reservations, just get the group leader's name, reservation number and birthday, and Disney will tie everyone's reservations together.

additional $15 fee is tacked on when dining at Palo, but the additional charge is worth it. The additional fee goes toward tipping the staff at Palo, who are not included in the regular dining rotation.

If guests choose not to dine at Palo's, they will take part in the rotational dining while aboard. Among the options:

The Animator's Palate: The walls of this restaurant slowly come to life throughout the evening. Classic Disney animations on the walls start out in black and white—matching the server's vests—and evolve into full color, dramatic renderings during the vivid finale. (*Among the offerings: Lobster and shrimp wrappers, duck and goat cheese flatbread, smoked salmon, gazpacho, Caesar salad.*)

Triton's: Located aboard the *Disney Wonder*, Triton's offers diners luxurious art deco surroundings and food with nautical flair. (*Among the offerings: Shrimp cocktail, leek and goat cheese quiche, tomato and basil soup, coquilles St. Jacques, beef tenderloin, baked duckling.*)

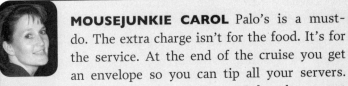

MOUSEJUNKIE CAROL Palo's is a must-do. The extra charge isn't for the food. It's for the service. At the end of the cruise you get an envelope so you can tip all your servers. That extra $15 is to tip the servers at Palo, who are not included in the envelope. It might seem like they're trying to squeeze another few bucks out of you, but the service at Palo is superior to the point of being ridiculous. It is very much worth it.

Lumiere's: Located on the *Magic*, Lumiere's allows guests to enter a grand dining room inspired by Disney's *Beauty and the Beast*. The cuisine follows suit, embracing a feel and taste particular to the French. (*Among the offerings: Deep-fried camembert fritters, escargot, chilled vichyssoise soup, beef tenderloin, roast duck.*)

Parrot Cay: A Bahamian setting, including a colorful motif reminiscent of the islands, welcomes guests who are invited to dine in more casual, carefree surroundings. (*Among the offerings: Spice Island chicken wings, baked crab, cold cream of mango and papaya soup, banana bread, beef rib eye, roast chicken, pan-seared grouper, baby back ribs.*)

Disney offers seven-night "land and sea" packages, where guests can spend three or four days in the theme parks, followed by three to four days aboard a cruise ship, depending on itineraries. With either, the key phrase, again, is convenience. When guests check-in to their resort hotel, they're provided with a Key to the World card. This card acts as a room key and a credit card of sorts, allowing guests to charge items to their room. Additionally, it becomes the stateroom key when the vacation switches into cruise mode.

> **TIP** *If you have suffered a blow to the head and make weird decisions like opting to work out while on vacation, the Disney Cruise Line can help you. (With the exercise, not the brain damage.) Guests determined to make us lazier folk feel bad can hit the gym, or take a run around the Deck 4 track, which is approximately one-third of a mile long.*

As he prepared to begin construction on Disneyland, Walt Disney said he wanted to create a place where parents and children could have fun together. While that philosophy has carried through to the Disney Cruise Lines, where the ships were constructed specifically with families in mind, teens and tykes are also provided with the opportunity to find some fun time on their own. Which, of course, leaves mom and dad with a little alone time. Read: Palo, deck chairs, fruity drinks, a locked door to the stateroom.

With nearly an entire deck dedicated to activities for younger travelers, parents can drop the little ones off and pursue their own seaborne happiness. The Disney counselor-to-child ratios are 1:15 for children ages three to four, and 1:25 for kids five to twelve. When dropping children under ten-years-old off, parents are given a pager, allowing them to relax and yet remain accessible if any needs should arise. Cast members are trained to deal with groups of children, and are always on watch for little wanderers. Safety is

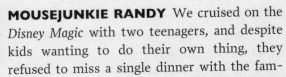

MOUSEJUNKIE RANDY We cruised on the *Disney Magic* with two teenagers, and despite kids wanting to do their own thing, they refused to miss a single dinner with the family. The servers treated them like gold. They made paper roses for the girls, and when they ordered Shirley Temples with extra cherries, they were presented with a glass full of cherries.

an important issue on Disney's cruise ships, and something cast members take seriously.

TIP *Feel free to just lay back and relax. Don't feel the need to plan anything. Just because there is plenty to do doesn't mean you have to do it all. Plus, there are far too many fruity drinks to sample and there is always an open deck chair somewhere.*

In the meantime, kids can choose from one of a number of age-specific programs: Kids three to seven can visit the **Oceaneer Club**—a play area designed to look like a pirate ship. Guests aged eight to twelve can spend time in the **Oceaneer Lab**—an interactive area where kids can have hands-on fun. A replica of the ship's bridge in **Ocean Quest** gives kids a chance to play Captain Stubing (or, perhaps more appropriately, Captain Jack Sparrow. No one under twenty-five would know Captain Stubing from Captain and Tenille.) Two teen-only spaces, **Aloft** (on the *Wonder*) and **The Stack** (aboard the *Magic*) give slightly older kids a place to retreat and feel more at home in a space designed to resemble a dorm room or apartment.

One night the girls couldn't decide on what dessert to order, so the server brought over a sample of every dessert. He continued to do that at every meal for the rest of the trip.

TIP   *If you're taking the family, book activities offered for the kids—that way the adults have a little time to enjoy each other's company alone.*

The options continue once the ship arrives at the Disney-owned Castaway Cay. The island is divided up into four beaches. There's **Castaway Family Beach** which offers families a chance to snorkel or play volleyball, **Scuttle's Cove**—for younger kids, **Teen Beach** (fairly self-explanatory) and the adults-only **Serenity Bay**.

 MOUSEJUNKIE CAROL Serenity Bay had a big bar and a beach. That's all I needed.

Fans of the *Pirates of the Caribbean* film series are also afforded a treat. Davey Jones' ghost ship, the *Flying Dutchman*, is anchored just off shore from Castaway Cay. Guests can get a fairly close up look at the full-size vessel, but onboard tours are not part of the offerings.

Guests can also choose from a number of Castaway Cay shore excursions, including a chance to interact with stingrays and some fantastic snorkeling opportunities.

TIP *Blue Tang fish—the basis for the character of Dory in Disney/Pixar's Finding Nemo are known to congregate near the Mickey Mouse statue in the island's snorkeling lagoon, providing fans of the movie (and people who like to look at blue fish) a chance for an up-close encounter.*

The leisure expert of the panel of Mousejunkies, Carol, has experienced spas all across Disney's properties. And while most are exemplary, the one-hour beach cabana massage has one element to it that keeps her from recommending it to visitors.

 MOUSEJUNKIE CAROL They oil you up big time. And what do you do from there? I showered after the massage, but they only offer you a rinse-shower. Even after rinsing off I was still covered in oil. I walked out into the sun and felt like I was baking. I could not handle the sun after being oiled up like that.

Guests not accustomed to vigorous massages may also not be prepared for the workout imposed on sore body parts. Masseuses locate pressure points and stress points and work them into submission. Their handiwork certainly accomplishes the goal, but sore muscles often follow.

Disney currently has two cruise ships in its fleet: The *Disney Magic*, which began sailing in July of 1998, and the *Disney Wonder*, which set sail about a year later. Each ship has 875 staterooms and differ very little in terms of design and feel.

The ships resemble a more elegant ocean liner style, with traditional round portholes and a classic design.

The *Magic* currently sails seven-day itineraries, which bring passengers to ports of call such as Castaway Cay, St. Maarten, St. Thomas, St. Croix, Tortola, Key West, Grand Cayman and Cozumel. The ship sailed to the West Coast in 2005 in honor of Disneyland's fiftieth anniversary, and made a transatlantic crossing in 2007, stopping in ports such as Barcelona, Cadiz, and Gibraltar.

In 2008, the *Magic* sailed a series of seven-night cruises from Los Angeles to the Mexican Riviera, before returning to Port Canaveral.

The *Wonder* sails both three- and four-night cruises, stopping in Nassau and Disney's own private island, Castaway Cay. The ship underwent a dry-dock rehab in 2006, adding a new toddler's pool, a giant, outdoor flat-screen TV near the Goofy Pool and expansions to the ship's spa and meeting facilities.

The *Wonder* and the *Magic* are both Panamax ships—the largest possible vessels that are still able to cross through the Panama Canal. In 2006, the Panama Canal Authority received support from about 78 percent of its electorate to embark on an expansion project. The expansion is expected to be completed by 2014 at a cost of $5.3 billion. After the expansion, the Panama Canal is expected to handle larger ships—something Disney Cruise Lines is planning for.

Disney Cruise Lines has announced the addition of two new ships to its fleet. The ships are unnamed at press time, but will each be two decks taller and slightly wider. Each of the new 122,000-ton ships will have 1,250 staterooms, and will be classified as Panamax II ships—able to cross through the Panama Canal only after the expansion project is completed. Until that time the ships, which are being built in Germany, will remain on the East Coast.

The two new ships are scheduled to launch in 2011 and 2012.

Disney Cruise Lines has also extended its contract with the Port Canaveral port authority for an additional fifteen years, has announced it will upgrade the area to accommodate the new ships, and will build a parking garage to accommodate more passengers.

(To book a vacation through Disney Cruise Lines, call 800-951-3532.)

Mousejunkies Marry

WHAT DOES A $20,000 ICE CREAM cone taste like?

Like mint chocolate chip. And fear.

Because when the ice cream was gone and I walked out of the Disney Vacation Club hospitality center one sunny morning in 2005, I was twenty grand lighter and had nothing tangible to show for it.

Sure, I'd be able to return to Walt Disney World twice a year for the next fifty years and not have to pay for a hotel, but you can't exactly pull that out of a box and show it to someone. It was a bit strange to lay out that kind of cash and not be able to hold on to something after.

Other than the ice cream, that is.

Despite a guarded approach and a general mistrust for timeshare salesmen, we gave in to my addiction and became owners of a real estate interest at Disney Vacation Club. At that point all it meant to me was that I'd be able to go to Disney World more often and I didn't have to mow the lawn at my "real estate interest."

I was soon to learn the intricacies of Disney Vacation Club — DVC to those who know the secret handshake. Specifically I began to learn how best to leverage what we had just bought,

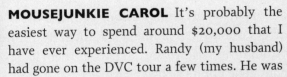

MOUSEJUNKIE CAROL It's probably the easiest way to spend around $20,000 that I have ever experienced. Randy (my husband) had gone on the DVC tour a few times. He was having a tough time convincing me that it was the way to go, so eventually he got me to go on a tour. (I will admit the free $100 in Disney dollars for taking the tour was my real enticement).

At the end of the tour, our salesman, Marshal (how many people fondly remember the name of the guy who convinced them to buy a timeshare) worked with us and talked about the different number of points we might want to buy. A quick 220 points later and we were out of there. Now I do think it was the best thing and the worst thing we have ever done. It's the best in that we do save money in hotels every time we visit. It's the worst, because, well, let's say that we tend to go more than our allotted 220 points will allow. So what do we do? We are now in a network where we will buy someone else's unused points for the year, transfer into our accounts and we're good to go one more time. DVC has really just been an instrument to bring us to Disney at least three times a year and if we can do so, four to five times a year.

how to visit our new second home most efficiently, and what it would mean for our family members and friends.

Disney Vacation Club is a timeshare-like operation, allowing members to buy a real estate interest through a one-time purchase of "vacation points." Members use points to pay for accommodations at one of the DVC resorts. Members can use the points, bank them for future use, borrow from future use years, or transfer them in or out of their account. The points renew every year.

When making a reservation, members are charged points. The number of points depends on what kind of room, what resort, and what time of year the reservations are for. Members can book a reservation at their "home resort" up to twelve months in advance, or at any other resort up to seven months in advance.

TIP *When booking a trip through DVC, stay at a cheaper hotel on weekends and pay cash. The point cost for weekends is astronomical and prohibitive. It's a smarter use of points to stay elsewhere and then transfer to your DVC resort after the weekend.*

That, in a nutshell, describes how I'll be spending the next fifty-nine years—which means I could potentially visit my vacation destination of choice ninety-eight more times. And optimistically, I'll be crippled and in a wheelchair on any vacation after 2037, so that's fifteen years of front-of-the-line privileges and getting on the bus first for this Mousejunkie.

I first became aware of the existence of Disney's Vacation Club in 1998. I considered it an interesting idea, but since we'd probably never come back it was something I never considered. Fifteen trips to Disney World later, the opportunity to take a DVC tour came up. And since it came with the promise of a $100 gift certificate, we thought we'd listen to the sales pitch, thank them for their time, and laugh about the whole experience while blowing $100 at Downtown Disney. Picking up a quick C-note on the Mouse wasn't a bad way to spend the morning.

Married to the Mouse

We scheduled our tour for 8 A.M.—thinking we could fly through the sales pitch, collect the cash, and then head out for the day. Early on the assigned morning we found ourselves in a blue DVC van, being carted to the Saratoga Springs sales center. The Saratoga Springs Resort—constructed on the site of the old Disney Institute directly across the waterway from Downtown Disney—was built to resemble the upstate New York horse racing mecca and spa retreat center of the early 1900s.

During the ride over, Amy kept elbowing me, saying, "We are *not* going to do this. We can *not* afford this. We are *not* going to do this."

"I know, I know," I said.

And I did know. But here's a little background that will come as no surprise to anyone: I always wanted to get in on DVC, if only because it would guarantee that I could come up with an excuse to get back to Disney World again. Plus it would take the sting out of the typical "last day of vacation" withdrawal—only because I knew we'd be back before too long.

We arrived at Saratoga Springs and were ushered into the lobby of the tour center. Under her breath, Amy kept saying, "No. No. No." But it was beautiful. The front desk had a waterfall behind it, everyone was smiling, and it was bright and spacious. Despite our supposedly united front against any kind of timeshare, I was already weakening.

We were ushered into a comfortable seating area, offered drinks and assigned to a guide named Bobby. I immediately put on my "anti-salesman" attitude. He was nice, but I'd rather cross some salesman I'd never see again than the woman I had to ride back in the van with.

We sat and talked for a while, and the strangest thing started happening—Amy started agreeing with Bobby. I kept a calm exterior, but on the inside I was freaking out. Unlike any other timeshare tour on the planet, it was very low-key. There were no high-pressure sales tactics and they didn't threaten to keep you locked up until you signed on the dotted line. It was an easy, pleasurable experience. By the time we got up to walk through the model units, it looked as if Amy's mind was made up. Still, I was extremely wary that she was just humoring him until the end, at which time she'd eviscerate the poor guy's pitch with her financially conservative weaponry. I was excited, but cautious.

We were walking back to the main office, and I was trying to make eye contact with Amy to see if she was agreeing for real, or being patronizing and evil, waiting to spring the big "no" on Bobby at some point. I was raising my eyebrows up and down, as if she'd be able to read that odd bit of facial communication and answer me in kind. I think she thought I was just being weird. The vibe I was getting, however, was that it made sense. Again, I was pleased, but still not ecstatic.

A few minutes later my questions were answered. He asked if we were interested. I looked at Amy and she said, "Well, he's going to keep coming back here, so I guess it makes sense."

I was officially engaged to Mickey Mouse. For the next fifty or so years, Disney World would be part of our lives. Our commitment was legally intended to last longer than most marriages. By the time our contract ran out I'd be in my mid-eighties, and my daughter would be looking forward to retirement in a few years. We'd all be traveling in air-locks and spending Space Bucks on our Dole Whips, no doubt.

We were then ushered into the closing room—a small office with a computer and a table. This is where we got down to brass tacks. We chose 200 points, our usage year started in June, and the points were available immediately. It was that simple.

Actually, it wasn't that simple. The time we took to fill out the paperwork gave Amy enough time to ruminate on the financial commitment we had just agreed to. There were a few ultimatums—namely: Stop buying bass guitars and forget about ever owning a motorcycle. I agreed.

And that was it. We were married to the Mouse. We were escorted to an ice cream shop designed to welcome new members, and perhaps provide the added benefit of easing the financial shock with a cone of cold, sugary opiates.

We had lunch at The Earl of Sandwich at Downtown Disney and talked over our totally unexpected investment.

MOUSEJUNKIE WALT When I go to Walt Disney World, I like to go for at least ten days, and DVC allows me to do that. And the fun thing is you start up a relationship with that corporation for the rest of your life. And while Disney is a big corporation, I don't think of it that way—mainly because of the way I'm treated while I'm there. When I first arrive at my resort for a vacation, I'm met by a cast member who always says, "Welcome home." And that pretty much sums everything up, because it feels that way when I go to Walt Disney World. I feel like I'm home.

I joined DVC in 2002. I fell in love with the Boardwalk Resort, and thought I could see myself going there every year. My grandmother had passed away the year before and my grandfather was not getting younger, so I thought it would be great to take my whole family down there. I was able to do that using DVC, and it was very rewarding. I knew after I went back one time, I'd want to go back many times in my life. It's the cheapest and best way because if feels like it's free. Of course you've already paid for it, but all you have to worry about is your flight, food, and park passes and you're all set.

It's also funny how contagious it is—how many people around you join once you take them. In my family alone we've got my aunt, my father, and a lot of friends who own at DVC.

Amy's happy but cautious outlook had evolved into just happy. We were making plans, talking about the future and figuring out a way to let our DVC traveling mates know we had taken the plunge.

We then took the $100 tour bonus and blew it all at the World of Disney store. I went in search of a shirt, watch or hat—something with the DVC logo on it. We had only been members for about two hours and I already wanted to flaunt it. I ended up trekking—and sweating—from the Boardwalk, to the Beach Club, to the Yacht Club and then back to the Screen Door shop on the Boardwalk. The best I could come up with was a beige DVC t-shirt. It would have to do.

For someone who returns to Walt Disney World quite often, Disney Vacation Club offers a chance to stay at deluxe-level resorts at a fraction of the rack-rate. The resorts range from quite nice to extravagant. Among them:

Old Key West: The first DVC resort built, Old Key West opened in the fall of 1991. The Lake Buena Vista Golf Course winds through its grounds, which reflect the feel of old Florida. Olivia's offers indoor and outdoor dining options right on the grounds. The Gurgling Suitcase bar sits on the pier overlooking the Sassagoula River, where guests can rent boats or hop a water ferry to Downtown Disney.

For the longest time I resisted staying at Old Key West, mainly because all I heard about it was that it was old and it cost the fewest number of DVC points to stay there. After a long weekend spent lodged there (and a few nights at the Gurgling Suitcase) I look forward to returning. The rooms are bigger, the resort is clean, it has a great ambience after dark, and it's an amazing value in terms of overall cost.

Beach Club Villas: Designed to feel like a New England seaside resort, the Beach Club shares access to Stormalong Bay—the best hotel pool on Disney property—with Disney's Yacht Club. The most important amenity at the Beach Club is its location: just a short walk to Epcot's International Gateway, and a quick boat ride to Disney's Hollywood Studios.

As a New Englander, do I think Disney's Imagineers accomplished their goal of creating a hotel that reflects a Cape Cod-style resort? No, not really. There aren't any scratch ticket stores on site. If they could staff the entire place with cast members named Sully or Fitzie and tuck a Dunkin' Donuts between the guard shack and the lobby, I'd say it'd come close though.

The Villas at Wilderness Lodge: Tall trees and thick woodlands surround this majestic resort, which is themed to look like a National Park Service lodge. The DVC villas are integrated into the resort, attached to the main lobby by a short walkway. A massive lobby welcomes guests, with rough-hewn exposed logs and an eighty-foot-tall fireplace dominating the space.

The Iron Spike Room boasts an impressive collection of Walt Disney's train memorabilia and deep, luxurious leather chairs in which to contemplate said collection. If you go at Christmas time, the lobby of this resort is worth a visit whether or not you are a guest there. A massive Christmas tree shoots up into the cavernous entryway, an impressive and festive display.

Boardwalk Villas: A favorite to almost anyone who stays there (or happens to walk through, see it on a postcard, or hear about it from a friend who saw it on TV), the Boardwalk is a true showpiece among Disney's resorts. Designed in the image of a turn-of-the-century Atlantic seashore hotel, the stately yet whimsical Boardwalk is among the most picturesque of all Disney's resorts.

The Boardwalk boasts its own entertainment district, with musicians, magicians, and showmen roaming the boardwalk (lower case "b") throughout the night, passing by one of the several restaurants and snack bars that dot the lakefront space.

While much of the nightly hubbub that goes on out in front of the guest rooms is filtered out, visitors will not be able to ignore the nightly fireworks at the adjoining Epcot theme park. Any thoughts of turning in early to get some rest will be sharply interrupted by the sound of IllumiNations going off nightly at 9 P.M.

Saratoga Springs Resort and Spa: The upstate New York horseracing destination has been faithfully recreated at the site of the former Disney Institute. A massive complex, Saratoga Springs Resort and Spa features themed pools, Victorian architecture, various springs, and fantastic views of Downtown Disney—which is located just across the lake. A short walk or ferry ride and you're right in the middle of the shopping, dining or people-watching action.

Not surprisingly, Saratoga Springs is a beautiful resort. The grounds are immaculate, the lobby is bright and clean, the main themed pool feels like a natural lake amidst large rock formations, and horse racing themes abound. It is a pleasure to stay at this resort.

That said, the bus service has been abysmal each of the three times I've stayed there recently. Long waits are the norm, and since the resort is so large it can take a good forty-five minutes to an hour to get to a theme park or restaurant. Plan to leave plenty of travel time when heading out for any scheduled plans. We usually end up breaking one of our cardinal rules if we stay at Saratoga Springs: We rent a car. I normally would never consider it, but being able to come and go when we want makes for a more convenient experience when the alternative is standing at a bus stop for forty minutes as the advanced dining reservation you made 180 days ago goes by.

Animal Kingdom Villas: The newest DVC resort, the villas are located both in the existing Animal Kingdom Lodge and in the new Kidani Village (which is slated for completion in 2009). The new units will more than double the current size of the resort and will include a children's water play area, a new restaurant, and its own savanna. A DVC spokesperson said the animals will slowly be acclimated to their new environment. Guests should not expect to see animals on the new savanna until sometime in the spring of 2009.

Staying at the Animal Kingdom Lodge is everything it's purported to be. A savanna-view room allows guests to start the day with a stunning view of animals in their natural habitat. Sunrises and sunsets explode through the lobby, bathing the authentic African art in a golden glow. One end of the massive, six-story lobby is glass-enclosed, providing a bright, naturally lit atmosphere.

Kingdom Towers/Bay Lake Towers/Whatever Tower: One of the worst kept secrets at Walt Disney World in recent years has been the construction of a new DVC resort attached to the Contemporary hotel called...Something.

For more than a year after ground was broken on the project, Disney refused to officially acknowledge the existence of the resort (despite the fact that, well, there it was), but documents submitted to the state of Florida indicated they planned to use the new tower for Disney Vacation Club.

The company took several missteps before officially unveiling the name for the project, but filings with the Florida Department of Business and Professional Regulation show it was at one time called "Kingdom Towers," and recently changed to the lengthy "Bay Lake Tower at Disney's Contemporary Resort."

Industry-watchers speculated that Disney was hesitant to announce the new DVC resort while it was still attempting to sell out the new Animal Kingdom Lodge property. A coveted Magic Kingdom-view is part of the new tower, making it the crown jewel of DVC's resorts. With construction nearing an end at press time, it stands as a moderately sized building just yards from the Contemporary Resort.

Disney Vacation Club also operates two off-site resorts: Disney's **Hilton Head Island Resort** in South Carolina, and

Disney's **Vero Beach Resort**, on Florida's Atlantic coast. Disney has recently broken ground on a newly planned Vacation Club resort in Oahu, Hawaii.

In each of the DVC resorts, guests can choose from one of four room types:

➤ A studio room is essentially a standard hotel room that can sleep four people.

➤ A one-bedroom vacation home has a master suite, living room, kitchen and a patio. The one-bedroom unit can sleep up to five people.

➤ A two-bedroom vacation home, also referred to as a two-bedroom lock-off, consists of a one bedroom unit and a second bedroom attached. A two-bedroom unit can sleep up to eight people.

➤ The grand villa is the granddaddy of all DVC units. It is luxury, convenience, and comfort all in one. The grand villa has three bedrooms, three baths, is a two-story unit and can sleep upwards of twelve people comfortably. While the Boardwalk grand villa is a one-story unit, and the Wilderness Lodge and the Beach Club do not offer grand villas, the top of the line unit at Old Key West is bigger than many private homes.

Renting the Secret

Disney Vacation Club counts more than 300,000 people among its members. Quite often, members end up with points they won't be able to use during a designated use-year. This glut is a bonus for visitors to Walt Disney World, who can rent points from members and stay at a deluxe resort for a fraction of the cost. The transaction, normally conducted completely online, requires a bit of trust, but it results in a much less expensive room rate.

The transaction works like this: The owner of the points—the DVC member—agrees to reserve a room in the renter's name in exchange for a cash payment. The trust element comes into play because the renter, assuming he or she is not a DVC member, has no control over the points. An unscrupulous DVC member could potentially play havoc with a trusting vacationer's plans and funds. While it has happened, it appears to be an uncommon occurrence. The average price-per-point rate ranges from $8 to $12, and sometimes slightly more.

TIP *Rent points from DVC members online to stay at a deluxe resort for less money. At an average rate of $10 per point, it would cost $80 per night (during the week) for the month of January to stay in a studio-sized room at the Old Key West resort. Visitors paying cash would pay $285 a night for the same room. Renting points would allow a guest to stay at the Villas at Wilderness Lodge during the same time period for an average of $120 a night. Guests paying cash would pay $225 to $385 a night for the same room. Arrange to rent points at sites such as dvcrequest.com, disboards.com, mouseowners.com, or dvctrader.com.*

In addition to reduced rates at deluxe-level hotels and an inflated sense of self-importance for belonging to a

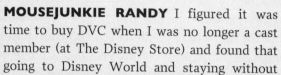

MOUSEJUNKIE RANDY I figured it was time to buy DVC when I was no longer a cast member (at The Disney Store) and found that going to Disney World and staying without discounts at a moderate resort, after years of staying at deluxe resorts, was not much fun. We also weren't going to be able to go as often, so we opted to buy.

As long as you're planning on making at least one trip a year, it's really a good value. If you intelligently figure out how to use the point system—avoid using points on weekends—it's an even bigger value. Plus you get to bring people with you who might not otherwise have the opportunity to visit Walt Disney World.

select group of dedicated Walt Disney World fans, there are members-only perks. DVC members enjoy discounts while shopping, dining, and booking entertainment and recreation options. The most valuable perk, however, is the reduced rate on an Annual Pass. Annual Passholders enjoy entrance to all four theme parks for one calendar year, access to special "Passholder-only" events, and occasional discounts on rooms, merchandise, and dining.

TIP *Will you be visiting a Walt Disney World theme park more than eleven days in a one-year period? If so, pick up an Annual Pass. DVC members enjoy a $100 discount.*

MOUSEJUNKIE J The reason we bought DVC was twofold. My wife Deb and I enjoy staying at higher-end resorts no matter where we go. Disney was no exception. After looking at rack rate prices and what DVC would end up costing us per year, it was a no-brainer. Owning DVC allows you to stay at higher end resorts cheaper than if you were paying cash. The driving factor for Deb was she loves the Boardwalk. If we always wanted to stay there, DVC was the cheaper answer. Do you want to go to WDW every year? Do you want to stay at higher-end resorts? If you answer these two questions "yes," then DVC is the answer.

Once we bought, there was never any buyer's remorse. Once we joined we also bought points at the Villas at the Wilderness Lodge. Then we bought at the Beach Club Villas, and now we own at the Boardwalk Villas.

The greatest value for us is that our choices are always nice resorts in great locations. The biggest regret was not doing it sooner. We bought when points were around $60-$70 a point. Right now they are well over $100. The prices will only go up, so waiting costs money.

Of the Mousejunkies—a group of eight people in total who travel to Walt Disney World several times a year each—there isn't one who doesn't belong to the Disney Vacation Club.

MOUSEJUNKIE WALT I don't understand why there isn't more DVC stuff to buy. DVC fans are the biggest fans of Disney and Walt Disney World and will eat up anything with Disney or a DVC logo on it. You'd think they'd put out a DVC catalog, but they don't. I go back every year and look for some new collectible or some new clothing with the DVC logo on it, but more often than not, it's the same old stuff year after year.

Mousejunkies Misbehave

IT WAS A LITTLE AFTER MIDNIGHT and I was dragging three pieces of luggage, a half-awake three-year-old, and an exhausted thirty-five-year-old through the front doors of Disney's Boardwalk Resort.

I was about to encounter an element of traveling to Walt Disney World that is as ever present as the quality of its service. I was about to stumble upon a Stupid Guest.

Even at that late hour, it was hard not to be impressed with the pristine condition of the hotel lobby. The hardwood floors were varnished to a high sheen, the oversized chairs looked incredibly inviting and a fire was burning cheerfully in the fireplace. The high ceilings, painted a bright white and done up with intricate carvings and odd knick-knacks, vaulted upward.

Those same ceilings also possessed remarkable acoustic qualities. How did I know? The minute we entered the main lobby to check in I heard a woman shrieking uncontrollably at the cast member behind the check-in desk.

In a shrill voice, she announced to anyone in the greater Orlando area that she wanted someone fired—immediately—because she didn't like the view from her room. The

woman was freaking out—at midnight—and wanted someone's head to roll.

Having been to Walt Disney World a few times by that
point, I'd seen my share of tantrums. In fact, I rated them,
graded them, and surreptitiously took photos of them. (I
thought this was funny until I had a toddler of my own.) But
this fit was a meltdown for the ages. Evidently she'd got a
"preferred view" room, instead of a "boardwalk view" room.
All her children had to look at was a "stupid golf course."
And due to this, the world was ending.

Yet the cast member could not have been calmer, more
accommodating and nicer to this shrill, spoiled personifi-
cation of evil. The cast member apologized, explaining that
while people can request certain views, they can never be
guaranteed, and she would do everything in her power to
make it better. However, this still wasn't good enough for
the midnight rambler on my left.

As she continued the tirade, I went through my check-
in process with another cast member who was quite good at
ignoring the verbal abuse being heaped upon his co-worker.
A few minutes later I was heading off to my room with that
woman's voice trailing behind me.

The funny thing is, I got a room with a great view.

The exchange between the enraged woman and the patient
cast member illustrated perfectly why we enjoy traveling to
Walt Disney World so often. The cast member maintained
a calm, cheerful demeanor and stayed focused on providing
top-notch service. It's something we've come to appreciate,
rather than expect. And it all took place while she was being
loudly and very publicly embarrassed.

It may have been the first time I'd witnessed such an exchange, but it was not the last.

Mayhem with Mickey

It's not always magic and pixie dust at Walt Disney World. There are examples of boorish guests, odd behavior and examples of the outrageous on every trip.

For some reason, people tend to forget basic rules of civil behavior when they drive beneath the giant welcome sign signals their arrival to Walt Disney World. The place can host some of the most heart-warming scenes imaginable, and yet it seems to draw some of the worst forms of humanity on the planet.

This occurs in part because when people travel to Walt Disney World their expectations are set quite high. Disney's reputation for customer service is legendary, and evidently this gives some ignorant guests the idea they can abuse cast members.

Threatening behavior is consistent enough where Disney cast members have a specific code for alerting security—a "1099." Calling a code 1099 means security is needed to handle an unruly, out of control, or physically abusive guest.

It's just another day in the life of a cast member working hard to make guests' dreams come true.

A few days after Miss Shrieky Shoutsalot tried to bully her way into a room with a better view, we had dinner at the Crystal Palace in the Magic Kingdom. It's a character buffet, where costumed Disney characters visit the diners one table at a time. If you sit patiently, the characters will make their way around the room. Diners will have a chance to visit with each of them.

As we took our seats next to a window facing Cinderella Castle, another family was brought in and seated at a table next to us. The man—loud, pushy, and sadly typical among those who are hot, hungry, and tired— grabbed a passing cast member gruffly by the arm and insisted the costumed characters deal with his kids immediately. Not when it was his turn—now. The character handler working the room asked them to remain seated, and the characters would make their way around to every table.

The man held tight to the cast member's arm and growled: "Give me your name please in case I decide to sue."

Yes. Sue. Over Winnie the Pooh. At Disney World.

Again, the cast members sprang into action. A manager was brought out, and within minutes the characters were huddling around their table. No doubt he was proud of kicking some Winnie the Pooh butt at Walt Disney World.

Sometimes, however, it just gets odd.

"I think this is gross and funny at the same time," a woman from England named Karen told me. "I saw a man walking toward me at the Magic Kingdom with white lycra cycling shorts on."

Things got very strange, very quickly.

"He had—how can I say this delicately—a rather large bulge in the front of his shorts. That's not all—it was all mis-shapen and knobby. Now, honestly, I don't make a habit of casting my eyes southward but this was just mesmerizing.

"As he walked closer the bulge got lower and lower until eventually a pair of socks fell out of the bottom of one of the legs. I doubled-up laughing and he went very red, took the socks all the way out and walked the other way."

There must've been something in the water when Karen visited Walt Disney World on that trip, because the oddities didn't end with Mr. Socky McCodpiece.

"One day I was walking near the Swiss Family Robinson tree house in the Magic Kingdom. I looked across the crowds and noticed a very large man lying against a grassy slope with no shirt on. He was only wearing a pair of shorts. That was fine, but the gross part came next.

"He had a hot dog sausage and was dipping it into salt— salt that he had poured into his huge belly button."

Unfortunately for the custodial staff at the vacation kingdom resort, tales of guests run amok are quite common. Guests may be overcome by the heat and feel nauseated, they may react poorly to Mission: Space and scream at their shoes, or they may have just dined at the ABC Commissary. Whatever the explanation, there seem to be bodily fluids flowing in the streets at Walt Disney World.

"My girlfriend Abby and I were leaving the park one night, when she turned to me and said, 'Oh, my God,'" Arissa Nelson, of Buena Park, California said. "I asked her what was wrong, when she pointed to a planter near the exit. There was a little boy standing in it.

"I asked Abby what he was doing. And she said, 'Look!' I looked again and the little boy was in the bushes peeing! When he was finished the little boy turned and said, 'I'm done, dad.'

"Let's just say that that was an interesting way to end our night."

There are restrooms scattered all over the theme parks and resorts. Just not in the middle of a decorative planter. But it seems to be reaching epidemic proportions.

While waiting for a ride to the Ticket and Transportation Center one night after closing at Epcot, a family came running up the ramp just as the monorail was about to leave.

"Hold that train!" the mother shouted at a cast member. "My son has to go to the bathroom and can't wait any longer."

Eyes rolled and roughly four hundred people groaned in unison. It was late, we were tired and it was time to head home. I had just spent the day trudging around the World Showcase, and there was a hotel pool howling my name. Still, an entire monorail filled with similarly exhausted guests was being held up because this woman decided she didn't want to wait for the next train.

She was outraged that there wasn't a bathroom on the monorail itself—I know this because she shouted it at the top of her lungs—and she insisted everyone be held up so she could take her kid to the public restroom back at the bottom of the ramp.

The woman was told the monorail was leaving, and another would be along in mere minutes. She glared at the cast member, mumbled something under her breath, and pushed her son onto the car behind ours.

The doors closed, the lights dimmed and we were on our way.

When we arrived at the Ticket and Transportation Center, the same woman sought out a cast member, jabbed her finger in his face and shrieked: "You should've held the train. I just let my son go to the bathroom in the cabin of your monorail. Have fun cleaning it up."

I don't know what it is about the monorail that attracts the psychotic element, but it might explain why the inside of the cars smell like goats. (For the record, cast members have attributed that smell to two specific things: Reconstituted air in the monorail's air conditioning system, and an adhesive used in the cars.)

I was walking near the monorail platform at the Polynesian one night when I saw a man poke his finger into a cast member's chest.

"You might want to call a janitor," he said.

The cast member asked him why. From the bullying look on his face, I knew the answer wasn't going to be, "Because I'd like to compliment him on the immaculate condition of this fine resort." Instead, the man snapped: "They wouldn't hold the train for us while my son used the restroom, so he left you a little present on the platform."

Indeed there was a gift deposited on the platform. It wasn't wrapped, but it's the thought that counts. The entire entrance side of the platform was blocked off, causing delays for the better part of an hour.

Sometimes it's not the guests' fault. Regardless, the results remain somewhat the same.

"My bid for the grossest guest trick was the amazing exploding diaper," confided a cast member who asked not to be identified. "Sad thing is, I really couldn't blame the guests for it. A

MOUSEJUNKIE CAROL We were celebrating my husband and friend's fortieth birthdays. We wanted to make reservations at a really nice restaurant, so we chose the Hollywood Brown Derby in Disney's Hollywood Studios. We were seated across from a gentleman—how can I describe him—dressed entirely in black with very long hair. He was seated alone and was facing us. It was just him—smack dab in the middle of one of the Brown Derby's circular booths. He just had a very odd vibe about him.

Throughout dinner I noticed the guy was absolutely shoveling food into his mouth. We had just finished our dinner and were awaiting the dessert menus, when the man picked up a plate with a half-eaten steak on it, leaned his face over it and proceeded to throw up everything he had just eaten.

I stood up and stared in shock. I must've gone completely white and bug eyed, because everyone followed my gaze and saw what was happening. And yet no one from the restaurant moved to help him. He leaned over and threw up some more. Luckily it was noisy in the

(Continued on next page)

family had a fully loaded diaper, and they put it on their stroller. (Thank you for not leaving it on a bench or table for someone else to find.) As they rolled along, it happened to bounce out. Before they could stop and pick it up, another guest just happened to step right in the middle of it, and—kaboom!

"Did you know that the average exploding diaper contaminates a radius of about eight feet?"

restaurant, because if I'd heard him gagging I think I would've reacted in much the same way. I would've lost it right there.

Our waiter came over and handed us our dessert menus.

You need to take care of the gentleman across from me," I told him.

The waiter took one look, threw the menus up in the air and ran off into the kitchen. Five to ten minutes passed, and the guy was sitting there throwing up and looking at it. Still, no one came by to help. Finally, a few minutes later the manager came by and threw a table linen over the whole scene so the restaurant patrons wouldn't have to look at it.

Our waiter came over and asked us if we wanted dessert. Seriously. I took one look at him and said, "I think we're done here. We've seen all we care to see."

As it turned out, the manager had to call a hazmat team to clear the scene. I understand cast members have to deal with what they call 'protein spills' all the time, but it's not a regular occurrence around our dinner table.

He rerouted the queue with a couple of ropes, sprinkled a whole bag of Voban, and waited for custodial personnel to arrive.

"All they could do is stare in disbelief and shake their head when I said, 'I'm going to need the big mop bucket for this one.'"

Wait, it gets better.

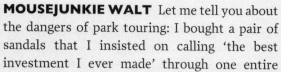

MOUSEJUNKIE WALT Let me tell you about the dangers of park touring: I bought a pair of sandals that I insisted on calling 'the best investment I ever made' through one entire Disney World trip. The people I was with got sick of hearing me say that, and it would come back to haunt me. I hadn't owned a pair since I was a kid, so just before the trip I went out and bought a pair and brought them with me.

When I got to Disney World I put those on and walked around. I loved them. And I had to keep saying it: 'These are the best investment I ever made.'

We were in Epcot, walking through the Canada pavilion when we got to the stone steps that lead up to the upper level. There was a baby sitting on the step, and as I went to step up, the baby darted in front of me. I tried to get out of way and my foot came down with a lot of force. The sandal went one way and my foot, which was driven into the jagged edge of stairs, went the other.

Still, I didn't step on the baby, so I didn't think anything of it. We continued to walk, and as that foot came forward I noticed a stream of blood sprayed out in front of me. I took another step and another spurt of blood shot out in front of me. It was then I realized how badly I was

(Continued on next page)

Sometimes it's surprising the lengths guests will go to in order to secure a good seat at one of the nighttime finale shows.

bleeding. I sat down and got a look at how deeply I was cut. I thought Mousejunkie Deb was going to pass out.

It was funny in a way, because I became an attraction for a bit. People were stopping and looking at all the blood. And it's also funny because you don't know who the managers and emergency responders are, but they are always there. In my case, they arrived on the scene within seconds. A woman came over—she was manager of the Canada pavilion—and a few seconds later EMTs were there. They put hydrogen peroxide on it, wrapped it up and suggested I go to the nearby hospital.

That was when I quite literally put my non-bleeding foot down. It was our last full day at Walt Disney World, and I wasn't about to spend it sitting in an emergency room. I signed a release saying I wouldn't sue Disney, they got me a wheelchair, and before too long we were back on track.

That's not to say I wasn't in pain, because I was. J had to push me around in the wheelchair. I thought I was going to be able to push the wheelchair by my own power, and I did for about fifty feet, but then my arms got tired and I let J push me around the park.

It's impressive how quickly the cast members responded and took care of me. They do a great job.

Shane Winters and her family were in line to watch Fantasmic! one night at Disney's Hollywood Studios. They were caught up in the crowd that usually gathers outside the theater, when chaos erupted. A man attempting to get through the mass of people knocked the family's six-year-old son to the ground, and threw a flying kick at the stroller a two-year-old was in.

"That was enough," she said.

The couple gave chase, but temporarily lost the thug. Minutes later, however, they spotted him sitting happily in a choice seat, waiting for the show to start. A quick call to security changed his plans.

Police arrived on the scene and pulled him out of his seat. His excuse for assaulting a young family on vacation at Disney World?

"He said we were blocking his way," Winters said.

Typical of Disney, things were made right.

"The park manager took us to an office backstage where we were treated like celebrities," said Winters. "He apologized for the man's behavior, gave us a behind-the-scenes tour, took us to the front of the line on all the attractions—people were trying to figure out if we were famous!

"At the end he gave us photos of all the attraction pictures. And then to make the night even better, he gave us passes to a VIP section for Fantasmic!, complete with free food and drinks. They went all-out with so much food—a waiter was there and we didn't have to lift a finger. We had so much fun, and it really made up for the man with the attitude. It's great to see how far Disney goes to make things right."

Sometimes no one means any harm, everyone is on their best behavior, and things still go wrong. Take, for example, the sad tale of Mousejunkie Walt. A Disney lover through and through, Walt was physically injured on two trips in a row.

But that wasn't the end of Mousejunkie Walt's adventures. A year later he was standing in line at Starring Rolls Café in Disney's Hollywood Studios. A woman standing in line in front of him turned quickly and spilled an entire cup of steaming coffee down his leg.

I watched it happen as if in slow motion, but from where I was sitting I couldn't see the seriousness of it until he limped painfully over to the table. His entire leg was glowing an angry red color. And again, Disney's cast members leapt into action. Within seconds workers arrived with cold compresses and a bag of ice. Meanwhile the coffee flinger paid for Walt's breakfast and begged forgiveness. Since we were in a Disney frame of mind—incredibly painful burns or not—Walt magnanimously let the woman off the hook.

"It was the very next trip after I cut my foot open," he said. "I swear I thought I was going to get hurt on every Disney trip from then on."

Thankfully, most of Walt's limbs remain intact, and he hasn't needed major reconstructive surgery. Yet.

Mousejunkies Confess

Why We Go

The sun was setting over Epcot as the park was just coming to life.

The sky was painted a vivid orange color over a cooling breeze that wafted in from the lagoon, carrying on it the sounds of swelling music. This was punctuated only by the staccato blasts of the Friendship horns as they ferried guests from one side of the World Showcase to another. A festive atmosphere filled the air and all around us families laughed, held hands and enjoyed the evening.

And yet I was miserable.

It was the final night of my first Disney World vacation as an adult. I had just spent a week in a place where every one of my expectations was exceeded, and within twenty-four hours I'd be very far away from it all. I had no idea when we'd be returning, and like a petulant five-year-old, I wanted to stomp my feet and refuse to leave.

Instead, like a petulant thirty-one-year-old, I opted to keep my mouth shut, take a few final pictures, and exert every ounce of energy I had not to explode in envy at every happy face I saw.

I had no way of knowing at the time that I had just taken the first step toward complete addiction, and that I'd be back standing in that very spot dozens of times in the next few years. All I knew was that I had been swept up in something very tangible, and it was about to go away.

The place has a way of sneaking up on the unsuspecting and ensnaring them in subtle yet enduring ways. There are a lot of arguments about why it works. I can only attest that it does work.

Maybe it's the carefully planned way you're plucked from reality and slowly immersed in a world with no cares. Maybe it's the music—how it slowly fills the background as you move from your everyday existence into a fantasyland come to life. It could be the architecture—recalling the romantic past or predicting a too perfect, exciting future full of hope.

At this point I know there are people who will scoff. Disney, to them, is a multinational conglomerate that only cares about separating mouth-breathing yokels from their vacation dollars. Call me naïve. Slow on the uptake. Blinded by commercialism. I'll cop to it. All I know is I bought into it and I'm glad I did.

As I mentioned earlier, the idea of having my dinner brought to me by adults making minimum wage dressed as fictional animals was the farthest thing from my mind when I first set foot on Disney property as an adult. And yet that's what happened. And somehow it had an affect on me.

Yet again, I'm not alone. Part of what attracts the Mousejunkies—and the many thousands of people who visit Walt Disney World multiple times—is that it makes you feel something. It's certainly not a passive, restful vacation. There's a great deal of planning and effort that goes into recreating in the Orlando area, if only because there are so many other people who are there alongside you (or in front of you) who want to do the same thing. It can take a certain amount of work to accomplish your vacation goals at Disney World. But the payoff can be huge.

Through the combined efforts of its creators, those who inherited the task of keeping it evolving, the cast members that keep it running and the guests who breathe life into it, Walt Disney World has become a place that can touch those who arrive inside its walls.

MOUSEJUNKIE JENNA Confession time— Main Street U.S.A. makes me cry. Sometimes it's big teardrops, and sometimes it's just a little water welling up in my eyes, but I always cry the first time I pass under the train station and find the Magic Kingdom unveiled before me. There is the town I always wanted to live in. There, in the distance, is the castle of little-girl dreams. And all around it is the kind of glamour and adventure you usually only experience on a movie screen, a vision of the future we're still waiting to come true, and the kind of candy-coated fun small children love and big kids secretly crave.

For me, Fantasyland isn't just one small section of the Magic Kingdom; it's the entire forty-seven square miles of land and everything in it. As soon as I pass under those gates, I feel both transported and transformed. I'm light and happy, and I feel like I'm home. But at the same time, I feel like I've run away from home, an escapee from humdrum reality. I have friends who wonder why I don't move to Florida and get a job with Disney. Maybe someday. I think I'd make a good "maid" at the Haunted Mansion. For now, though, Disney is my Fantasyland, my Laughing Place, my escape hatch. I hope it stays that way forever, and I hope Main Street always makes me cry.

Most people just smirk when I tell them I'm going to Walt Disney World. Most of them get it, but they don't *really* get it. People think of the cost and the crowds and don't see why I consider a year without a Disney trip a barren twelve-month wasteland.

Only one person has really been confused and derisive. Each time I'd mention Disney World, he'd say 'Oh, you're going with your little niece?' Knowing, of course, that I didn't have a niece and I would be going alone or with other adults. He never missed an opportunity to point out that it was very expensive and I'd just gone the year before. Finally, I asked him about his yearly trips to Las Vegas. Did he go with friends? Did the Strip really change that much every year? How much did he usually spend on a trip? When he told me, I pointed out the similarities in our touring styles, even if they were vastly different vacation spots, "You have Vegas. I have Disney." After that he stopped bothering me.

My parents love it and encourage me to go. They know I get antsy if I don't have a trip planned. They've

(Continued on next page)

also reaped the benefits of me being a Mousejunkie, because when we travel together they know it's going to be a well-planned trip. My siblings are tolerant, but not enthusiastic. My brother doesn't like to plan anything in advance, so he's not very interested. My sister is actually going on her first trip since 1986 soon, and though she's not as interested as I am, she listens attentively to my descriptions and tips.

My dream scenario would be getting my whole family down to Disney World for a family vacation. I would love to have enough DVC points to book a two-bedroom villa for me and my parents and a couple of studios for my siblings and their families (a grand villa may sleep twelve, but it's too small for my family and their personalities). My dream is to be able to share WDW with the people I love.

I think I have always loved Walt Disney World. I was born the year it opened, so that may be the source of some of my attachment. I have literally grown up with Disney World. However, the first time I ever felt that Disney was my second home was the first day of my first trip as an adult. I was meeting a friend on that trip, but was solo for the first two days. The day I arrived, I visited the spa at what was then the Disney Institute, had an early dinner with an aunt who lived nearby, and unexpectedly found myself back in my room with nothing to do by 8 P.M. That certainly wouldn't do—not with an Annual Pass voucher burning a hole in my pocket. So I took a bus over to the Magic Kingdom and planned to head straight to It's a Small World.

As I passed under the train station, I realized that the Main Street Electrical Parade was passing through. A giant pink elephant was the very first thing I saw. I couldn't help it—I was instantly in tears. I was home.

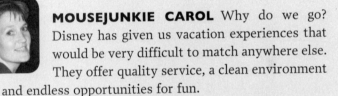 **MOUSEJUNKIE CAROL** Why do we go? Disney has given us vacation experiences that would be very difficult to match anywhere else. They offer quality service, a clean environment and endless opportunities for fun.

But the real reason I go is that I love being a kid. My family is always playing board games or card games at every gathering. We do not just sit around and have intellectual conversations. We sit around a table and break out the games—Mouse Trap (sorry Mickey) and Build a Better Mouse Trap. Walt Disney World is just my big board game.

I am one of seven siblings, so a trip to Walt Disney World was too costly for that size of a family—until 1993, that is. We were sitting around talking when it was mentioned that the family never took a big trip together. My mother's wheels were turning as she was listening to her children obsessing about a trip. The next day she took a look at the family finances and said: "We only live once. It's time for a trip to Disney World."

She had booked a trip for a total of fifteen people. We stayed at a Days Inn on International Drive, which

(Continued on next page)

isn't exactly the top hotel, but with that many people we didn't care.

The first time I ever walked into the Magic Kingdom was with two of my brothers and my now-husband Randy. Our first Florida experience was waiting in line to go on Splash Mountain. We were waiting patiently, when an infamous Florida rain shower hit. All around us people in line whipped out their ponchos, while we just stood there like the Disney virgins we were. We had no idea about the fast-changing, unpredictable Florida weather, so we just stood there getting soaking wet. By the end of the ride the park was a nice shade of yellow as everyone at that time was sporting the poncho.

That entire week was such a whirlwind, but it ended up being one of the best times my family has ever experienced together. I hope someday I can return with the family (maybe a bit older, but I'll always feel like the kid.)

Randy and I enjoyed the experience so much that it keeps us going back there again and again. By the end of that week we had already determined that Walt Disney World would be where we would spend our upcoming honeymoon.

I could go on about family gatherings as I have been fortunate enough to expose other family members to this wonderful experience. My ultimate goal would be to bring down the entire family to re-create that first great trip.

MOUSEJUNKIE DEB When people ask why we go so often, I try to explain, but unless I'm talking to another Walt Disney World fan it's just too hard.

People have a lot of preconceived ideas about it, especially if they've never been, because they base their opinions on what comedians, cartoons, and general folklore espouse without really knowing or experiencing it. Disney is not perfect, but it's pretty darn impressive. I consider myself a well-adjusted, semi-intelligent, reasonably traveled individual, but when I try to convince a non-believer of the magic, I may as well hang up my Ears. I suddenly become part of the marketing machine to them.

The only way to get it is to experience it, opening yourself up to the thoughtful, created environment it's fashioned to be. Of course it's not real life. Of course there's a man who's got to file his taxes inside the Eeyore costume. Of course you're not *really* on an African safari, or road testing the next GM model. Of course the elevator isn't really going haywire in the tower. But while you're there, away from *your* real life, if you can immerse yourself in the show, and appreciate everything that goes into making that show appear to be your reality while you're there—from the marketing genius to the cast member dedication that makes it possible—you'll get it.

For the rest, I just tell them I'm going to Florida.

MOUSEJUNKIE WALT I'm always accused of being a big kid. At work I'm known as being the joker. So when I go to Walt Disney World, I can be a kid again.

It's more than that though. I have this overall feeling when I get there of overwhelming happiness. Not that I don't have a good life outside of Walt Disney World, because I do. But when I'm there, there are no problems. There's so much going on and so many things to do and see, you immerse yourself in it. You don't have time to think about your outside life the entire time you're there. It can get to the point where you don't even see cars. It's one big fantasy dream come to life.

You've also got so many choices. No matter how many times you go, it's never the same trip twice. You can go on rides, see all the shows like Festival of the Lion King or Flights of Wonder, you can see the fireworks displays every night—Wishes, IllumiNations or Fantasmic—there are a million amazing things to do.

For example, one trip you're a child. You go to all the attractions, ride the roller coasters, visit the characters. The next trip you don't do any of that. You sit at the resort, sleep late, play golf and go out to clubs.

It's all things to almost all people. You can make your trip whatever you want it to be.

Some people say it's an exhausting place to vacation. And in some respects they're right. But I've found that it works like this: If you go someplace like Aruba, you come back and your body is relaxed, but not your

(Continued on next page)

mind. You have plenty of time to lie on the beach and do nothing—and your mind is still working away thinking about what's going on back home. If you go to Walt Disney World, you come home and your body might be tired, but your mind is totally relaxed and rejuvenated. You completely check out of your normal life. There's so much stimulation and so much to see and hear and taste and think about, that you don't have any time at all to dwell on any stress you might be having at work back home or anything like that.

To a large extent I'm a creature of habit. There's a comfort to going and knowing it, but the thing I like most is bringing new people. It's fun to go with friends, but when you go with someone who has never been, it's just like experiencing Christmas with young kids. There's a whole new and exciting aspect to it.

When you go to Disney World, you have to realize it's not solely about crazy thrill rides. What makes Disney so special is how they immerse you into the theming. Expedition Everest is great, but walking around and seeing all the artifacts they brought back from Tibet is what makes it so believable and great. When you go on Dr. Doom's Fear Fall across town at Universal's Islands of Adventure, there's no theme at all. It's one of my favorite rides, but it goes like this: They strap you in, they shoot you up, it scares the life out of you and it's over. It's a thrill, but that's it. At Disney World it's all about the details and the theming and giving you a chance to leave all your worries and stress at home. At least for a little while.

MOUSEJUNKIE J There are few things in life that one can call guaranteed winners. For me, Walt Disney World is guaranteed to be a great time, every time.

The accommodations, no matter what level of room, are always cool, clean, and inviting. The ice cream and other treats always taste better when you are standing on Main Street USA. The Rock 'n' Roller Coaster will always take my breath way. Vacations at Walt Disney World are consistently fun and memorable. Some people may like the adventure of booking a hotel room unseen in a country that is questionable in its safety. I like knowing ahead of time that I will be having a good time with no worries. Disney World gives me that security.

People who go to Walt Disney World more than a few times (people like the Mousejunkies) also know that it is not the same boring place if you know what to do. No trip is ever the same and we *always* find something new each time we go. There are always examples of a cast member going out of his or her way to make your trip special.

"Other than the occasional three-year-old meltdown, everyone is always smiling or looking at the sites in awe. I do not have to worry about what to wear because there is always someone not ten feet away wearing something I would not be caught dead in. It gives me comfort. I like being comfortable and relaxed on vacation. That is what taking a vacation is all about. Now if I could only get my wife to leave the work-issued Blackberry at home, we'd be all set.

MOUSEJUNKIE RANDY It's a fantasy world. And yet at the same time you always know what you're going to get—a really great experience. Disney uses the phrase "Where Magic Lives" to describe itself, but it's true. They do a great job trying to maintain that 'magic.'

There's a comforting familiarity about the place that I like too. For someone who grew up watching *Wonderful World of Disney* on TV on Sunday nights, it's a place where you can relive those days and then you can go and live in that world.

You don't have to see everything or do everything to have fun there. It's the sights, the sounds, the smells that make it special. It's the 'show' as they call it at Walt Disney World. It's always going, and you can always experience it.

Like the other Mousejunkies, I usually face the requisite questions just as we're preparing for another visit: "Don't you get bored?" (No.) "How many times is enough?" (At least one more time, evidently.) "You're going to give them more of your money?" (It's just money.) "Don't you want to see anywhere else?" (I already have. And I will again.)

But the most common question: Why do you go?

When I'm asked that I usually say how it's a quick flight, it's easy, the cast members treat you like royalty or how we've learned to vacation there rather affordably. That's all true, but the real answer goes deeper. I go back for the chance to feel like a kid again. To walk the same path I first walked with my grandmother decades earlier. To put my arm around Amy in the dark of the Haunted Mansion. Again. To see the look on my daughter's face as she sees her dreams literally come to life. To eat too much, drink too much, and to laugh too much. To see other people laugh too much.

To be taken back to an idyllic resort aboard a slow boat under a clear sky. And to hold my daughter's hand the next day as together we watch a fairy tale castle emerge from the gauze of an early morning fog. And yet while there's nothing quite like seeing a Disney World theme park awaken first thing in the morning, clean and new, it's at the end of the day when they really start to come alive.

The park's heart pulses through the twinkling lights that come to life as the sun sets, bathing guests in a golden glow.

Music—playful and lilting, subtle and stirring, moving and majestic—blankets the perfectly manicured grounds, guiding visitors through cobblestone streets, nostalgic sidewalks and rough-hewn paths.

Wandering from the fantastic to the inspiring, guests eventually find themselves at the foot of a massive tree made more majestic by the animals that populate its surface, standing beneath a gargantuan sorcerer's hat overflowing with magic, within a futuristic sphere reflecting the past and pointing the way to the future, and dreaming in the shadow of a perfect castle straight out of a storybook.

And ultimately they find themselves in the playground of one man's creativity, drive, and imagination.

Walt Disney World provides top-notch service when many service and hospitality industry workers exude disdain for customers. It allows adults to drop their guard and feel like kids again. It offers hope in an unsteady world. And it has evolved into what Walt Disney hoped his original theme park would become—a place where age relives fond memories of the past, where youth savors the challenge and promise of the future. It's a place dedicated to the ideals, the dreams, and the hard facts that have created America, and it has become a source of joy and inspiration to all the world.

Glossary

Mousejunkies—people who are obsessed with all things Walt Disney World—can sometimes seem to have their own language. Acronyms, nicknames, and shortened versions of longer titles pepper their conversations. Venture onto any Disney-related online community and you'll be overwhelmed by Mousejunkie-speak.

To help readers navigate the pixie dust-clouded waters of Disney lingo, here is a glossary of some of the more common terms found in this book and often used in online Walt Disney World correspondence:

ADR: Advanced Dining Reservations. Guests who call to reserve a dinner reservation are actually making an Advanced Dining Reservation. To make an ADR, call 1-407-WDW-DINE.

All Star Resorts: The term "All Stars" refers to three of Disney's value level resorts—All Star Music, All Star Sports, and All Star Movies. The three resorts are located next to one another near Disney's Animal Kingdom theme park.

Animal Kingdom Lodge: A deluxe-level resort that opened in 2001, the Animal Kingdom Lodge (AKL) is situated around a savannah where giraffes, zebras and other wild animals graze.

Bay Lake: A lake located to the east of the Magic Kingdom and just behind the Contemporary Resort. It connects to the nearby Seven Seas Lagoon. Fishing excursions, parasailing, and boating activities are offered on Bay Lake.

Beach Club: The Beach Club Resort (BC) is a deluxe-level resort located near the Epcot theme park. It is themed to look like turn-of-the-century seaside Atlantic cottages.

Boardwalk Resort: The Boardwalk Resort (often shortened to BW, BWI for Boardwalk Inn, or BWV for Boardwalk Villa), is a deluxe-level resort designed to look like a 1920s Atlantic boardwalk.

Caribbean Beach Resort: A moderate-level resort opened in 1988, the Caribbean Beach Resort (CBR) is located near Epcot and features a Caribbean theme throughout. The buildings encircle a small lake called Barefoot Bay.

Contemporary Resort: One of the original resorts at the Walt Disney World resort, the Contemporary (CR) was built using modular construction. Pre-built rooms were placed into the building's frame by a crane. A bit of trivia: President Richard Nixon gave his "I'm not a crook" speech at the Contemporary Resort in 1973.

Coronado Springs Resort: Opened in 1997, this moderate-level resort has a southwestern theme and features a pool in the shadow of a Mayan pyramid. Coronado Springs Resort (CSR) has a large convention center and often hosts trade shows.

Disney's Animal Kingdom: The fourth theme park built at the Walt Disney World resort, Animal Kingdom (AK) opened in 1997.

Disney's Hollywood Studios: The third theme park built at the Walt Disney World resort, it was opened as Disney-MGM Studios in 1989. The name was changed to Disney's Hollywood Studios (DHS) in January of 2007.

Disney's Magical Express: Guests staying at a Walt Disney World resort can use Disney's Magical Express buses (ME) to travel from Orlando International Airport to their resort for free.

Disney Vacation Club: Often referred to simply as "DVC," Disney Vacation Club is essentially a vacation timeshare, allowing people to purchase a real estate interest in one of the DVC resorts. Members purchase points which are used to make reservations at a DVC resort. The points are renewed annually.

Dolphin: The Walt Disney World Dolphin hotel is located in the Boardwalk resort area. It is operated by Starwood Hotels and Resorts Worldwide under the Sheraton Hotels brand. It is decorated in "Floribbean" style, using nautical themes in varying shades of pink and coral. It is adjacent to the similarly-themed Walt Disney World Swan hotel.

Downtown Disney: An outdoor shopping, dining, and entertainment complex at the Walt Disney World resort. It features several themed and chain restaurants like the Rainforest Café, House of Blues, and Planet Hollywood, as well as the Cirque du Soleil theater where *La Nouba* is performed. Downtown Disney (DTD) is divided into three sections: the Marketplace, Pleasure Island, and the West Side.

Epcot: The second theme park built at the Walt Disney World resort, Epcot opened in 1982. Originally named Epcot Center, its name was shortened to Epcot in 1994.

Extra Magic Hours: One of the Walt Disney World theme parks opens early or stays open after regular park closing hours every day. Guests staying at a Walt Disney World resort can take advantage of Extra Magic Hours (EMH), enjoying, in theory, shorter wait times and lighter crowds.

Fastpass: Disney's Fastpass (FP) is a virtual queuing system wherein guests insert their park tickets into a kiosk that then distributes a small ticket with a return time stamped on it. Guests return to that specific attraction at the prescribed time, thus bypassing the sometimes lengthy standby line. Guests are allowed to have only one Fastpass per park ticket at one time.

Fort Wilderness: A resort with campsites that allow guests to tent, use their own camper or recreation vehicle, or stay in a cabin. Fort Wilderness (FW) opened just weeks after the Magic Kingdom in 1971.

Friendship Launch: These are the boats that shuttle guests around the Epcot theme park and resort area. The Friendships travel from one side of the World Showcase Lagoon to the other, and from the Boardwalk area resorts—including the Boardwalk, Yacht Club, Beach Club, the Swan and Dolphin hotels—to Epcot and Disney's Hollywood Studios theme park.

Grand Floridian: Disney's Grand Floridian Resort and Spa (GF) is a deluxe-level resort across the Seven Seas Lagoon from the Magic Kingdom. Its look was inspired by the beach resorts of Florida's East Coast.

Hoop-Dee-Doo Musical Review: A dinner show held at Pioneer Hall on the grounds of Fort Wilderness, the Hoop-Dee-Doo Musical Review (HDDMR) is a Wild West vaudeville review. The shows run approximately two hours.

International Gateway: A "back door" entrance to the Epcot theme park, the International Gateway is accessible through the Boardwalk area resorts. Entering through the International Gateway puts visitors into the United Kingdom pavilion in the World Showcase.

Kidcot Fun Stops: There are sixteen Kidcot Fun Stops located in the Epcot theme park throughout Futureworld and the World Showcase. Children are given a cutout mask which they can color and decorate as they stop at each of the locations throughout the park. Cast members will also stamp the mask at each country or Kidcot Fun Stop.

Magic Kingdom: The Magic Kingdom (MK), which opened in 1971, was the first theme park at the Walt Disney World resort.

Magic Your Way: What Disney calls its theme park tickets. Guests can buy the base Magic Your Way ticket, or add several options, such as Park Hopping or No Expiration.

Mousejunkie: Anyone interested in or obsessed with Walt Disney World. Someone of high standards, great knowledge, a sense of humor, a yearning for fun, and is normally extremely attractive and intelligent.

Old Key West: The original Disney Vacation Club resort, Old Key West (OKW) opened in 1991 and evokes a Key West theme.

Park Hopping: The act of leaving one Walt Disney World theme park and going to another in a single day is called Park Hopping. Guests must have the Magic Your Way Park Hopper option in order to move between two or more theme parks in one day.

Pop Century: A value resort, Pop Century has 2,880 rooms in ten separate, themed buildings.

Polynesian: Disney's Polynesian Resort (often referred to in shorthand as "the Poly"), opened in 1971 on the shores of the Seven Seas Lagoon. It reflects a Hawaiian theme, and is one of the original Magic Kingdom area resorts.

Port Orleans French Quarter/Riverside: A moderate-level resort, the French Quarter (POFQ) and Riverside (POR) were once two separate resorts. They were combined in 2001.

Saratoga Springs: The Saratoga Springs Resort and Spa (SSR) is located across the Lake Buena Vista Lagoon from Downtown Disney, and was built to look like the upstate New York spa and horseracing town. It is the largest of the Disney Vacation Club resorts.

Seven Seas Lagoon: The man-made body of water located in front of the Magic Kingdom.

Spaceship Earth: The geodesic sphere (the giant golfball) that functions as the Epcot theme park's icon, Spaceship Earth (SE) stands 18 stories tall and houses a thirteen-minute dark ride that takes guests through the history of human communication.

Swan: The Walt Disney World Swan hotel is located in the Boardwalk resort area. It is operated by Starwood Hotels and Resorts Worldwide under the Sheraton Hotels brand. It is decorated in "Floribbean" style, using nautical themes in varying shades of pink and coral. It is adjacent to the similarly-themed Walt Disney World Dolphin hotel.

Tree of Life: A 14-story artificial tree that acts as Disney's Animal Kingdom's park icon. Images of more than 325 animals are carved into its trunk, and the structure houses a 3-D movie, *It's Tough to Be a Bug.*

TTC: The Ticket and Transportation Center is located between the Magic Kingdom parking area and the Seven Seas Lagoon. At the TTC you can board a monorail to Epcot or the Magic Kingdom, or a ferry boat to the Magic Kingdom. The Magic Kingdom Kennels are also located there.

Wilderness Lodge: Disney's Wilderness Lodge Resort (WL) is a deluxe-level resort on the shores of Bay Lake. It look was inspired by the great lodges of the Pacific Northwest.

World Showcase Lagoon: The body of water around which Epcot's World Showcase is situated. Epcot's IllumiNations: Reflections of Earth show is displayed over the World Showcase Lagoon nightly. The World Showcase Lagoon has a perimeter of 1.2 miles.

Yacht Club: Designed to look like a New England seaside retreat, the Yacht Club (YC) is located in the Boardwalk area near the Epcot theme park.

Index

Acknowledgments

These travelogues, anecdotes, tales, and experiences could not have taken place without the assistance and camaraderie of many people. I would like to thank the following: the tireless, talented, and patient Mousejunkies—Randy and Carol Houle, J and Deb Cote, Walt Pomerleau, and Jenna Petrosky. Amy Burke (the reluctant Mousejunkie,) Katie Burke (the newest Mousejunkie,) Bill and Karen Burke, Connie and David Bartlett, Ryan Elizabeth Foley, Julian at Mickeyxtreme. com, Barry Kane, Adam Powers, Charles Stovall, Carol Henderson, Dorothy Burke, who first showed me the way to the Castle and left us while we were there, and God.

About the Author

Bill Burke is a journalist with eighteen years experience in the newspaper and magazine business. A dyed-in-the-wool New Englander who recently came to the conclusion he hates the cold weather but can't live without good fried clams, Bill spent portions of his childhood living in different parts of the country and traveling throughout the United States. His family then returned to the northeast where he remained until discovering the joy of having his meals served by adults dressed as fictional characters. Now he flees to the warm embrace of central Florida whenever time and finances allow. Or even if they won't.

After trying out a number of different career options ranging from installing concrete foundations and digging ditches to working as a bouncer at an oceanfront nightclub and selling sci-fi collectibles, he stumbled across journalism. In the ensuing years he has covered marathons and murders, and written everything from business features to comic book scripts. He has been a cops-and-courts reporter, written features, interviewed musicians and actors, and worked as a travel writer. He was the online managing editor for the *Boston Herald* for six of the eleven years he spent at that newspaper. Bill has been traveling to and writing about Walt Disney World for the past ten years.

Bill plays bass guitar in a blues band, Irish music on the tenor banjo and mandolin, and bagpipes when he wants to annoy his wife of thirteen years. He has considered moving to Florida, but has been told that the state lacks good Chinese food. He lives in southern New Hampshire with his wife, Amy, and six-year-old daughter, Katie.